ALFRED DREYFUS

Alfred Dreyfus

The Man at the Center of the Affair

MAURICE SAMUELS

Yale

UNIVERSITY
PRESS

New Haven and London

Yale University Press books may be purchased in quantity for educational,
business, or promotional use. For information, please e-mail sales.press@yale.edu
(U.S. office) or sales@yaleup.co.uk (U.K. office).

Set in Janson Oldstyle type by Integrated Publishing Solutions.
Printed in the United States of America.

ISBN 978-0-300-25400-6 (hardcover : alk. paper)
Library of Congress Control Number: 2023938315
A catalogue record for this book is available from the British Library.

This paper meets the requirements of ANSI/NISO Z39.48-1992
(Permanence of Paper).

10 9 8 7 6 5 4 3 2 1

Frontispiece: Police identification photograph of Alfred Dreyfus
(after degradation), 1895; albumen-silver print, 3 1/8 × 2 4/6 inches (Gift of
Mr. and Mrs. Herbert D. Schimmel, 1990-134; photo by Richard Goodbody;
courtesy of The Jewish Museum, New York/Art Resource, New York)

For my father, Richard A. Samuels (1928–2021)

CONTENTS

ALFRED DREYFUS

---◆◆◆◆---

Introduction

ALFRED DREYFUS would not have wanted to be the subject of this book. Shy, serious, ill at ease outside his family circle, he rarely voiced his opinions on political matters. But through no fault of his own, he was thrust into the center of a controversy that divided the French nation and riveted the world. An ardent patriot, he was accused of committing treason. A law-abiding citizen, he suffered a colossal injustice. A discreet Jew, he became the emblem of antisemitic persecution. Rarely has so private a person been forced to live so public a life.

At the end of the nineteenth century, the heyday of the mass press, multiple newspapers competed for attention in capital cities across the globe, and Dreyfus's story made for very good copy: accused of selling military secrets to Germany, denounced by antisemites, found guilty on trumped-up evidence, deported to a brutal island prison off the coast of French Guiana, proven innocent by the efforts of his devoted family, defended by France's leading intellectuals, brought back for a second trial, found guilty again, pardoned, eventually exonerated and awarded the Legion of Honor for his trouble. It is not hard to see why Dreyfus's life has served as fodder for countless novels, plays, movies—even comic books—over the course of the past century.

It is also not hard to see why it has given rise to more scholarship than almost any other event in French history. The Dreyfus Affair plunged France into a political crisis because it raised fundamental questions about the nature of liberal democracy— the form of government that guaranteed rights to the individual through the rule of law. It raised these questions at a moment when liberal values were triumphing throughout much of the world, but also when the seeds of anti-liberalism were being planted in many of the same nations that had pioneered political freedom. On its face, the affair asked whether individual citizens could claim the right to impartial justice even when this right conflicted with military or national interest. On a deeper level, it asked whether religious and racial minorities belonged in the nation at all.[1]

Scholars have thoroughly explored the ins and outs of Dreyfus's legal case as well as dozens of other topics related to the affair. They have shown how it widened divisions between left and right in France, led to the separation of church and state, witnessed the first interventions by intellectuals in political matters, and even changed social and gender relations in lasting ways. Surprisingly, however, the Jewish dimension of the affair has received relatively little attention. Although everyone knows that Dreyfus was Jewish—often it is the *only* thing that people know about the case—the role that Dreyfus's Jewishness played both for him and for his opponents has rarely been the focus of study. And the profound effect of the affair on Jews around the world has gone almost completely unexamined.

This hesitation dates to the early days of the affair itself, when Dreyfus's family and other supporters, many of them Jews, feared that speaking out against antisemitism would only fan the flames of that hatred. They also wanted to avoid seeming to support Dreyfus merely out of sectarian impulses, and to give the lie to accusations by antisemites that Dreyfus was defended by a powerful "Jewish syndicate." Instead, they sought to broaden their coalition by emphasizing the universal issues at stake in the case—truth, justice, the rule of law, et cetera.[2]

Ever since, scholars, especially in France, have shared this tendency to universalize the affair. Much of the scholarship on the case treats the issue of antisemitism only tangentially. And some scholars even go so far as to deny the importance of antisemitism to the case. There has been a corresponding reluctance, especially by those sympathetic to Dreyfus, to explore his Jewishness—perhaps because his enemies harped upon it for so long. Indeed, it is not a coincidence, given the French tendency to downplay the Jewish angle, that the one work to discuss Dreyfus's Jewishness unabashedly is by an American researcher.[3]

To write a "Jewish life" of Dreyfus is therefore something of a provocation, or at least a challenge to conventional historiography. The more I have delved into the affair, however, the more I have realized that Jewishness was central to almost every aspect of it. But what does writing a "Jewish life" of Dreyfus entail?

It means, first, exploring the role of Jewishness in Dreyfus's life and that of his family. As will become clear, this is not a straightforward proposition. Dreyfus was not a spiritual or religious person. He rarely spoke of God in either his personal or public writing. He also rarely evoked what we would call today his "Jewish identity." This was partly a result of his rationalism, his scientific worldview, but it also reflects a very specific way of being Jewish that emerged in France in the nineteenth century, which prioritized public displays of French patriotism and relegated religion to the private sphere.

Dreyfus is often referred to as an "assimilated Jew," but this is a label that I prefer not to use in his case because it connotes rejection of the minority culture in order to join the majority one. Neither Dreyfus nor his family sought to disavow their Jewish origins. On the contrary, it was Dreyfus's refusal to hide or downplay his Jewishness that attracted the negative attention of certain of his military superiors and that was at least partly responsible for the accusations against him. A major part of this book, especially the early chapters, involves explaining how Dreyfus and his family embraced a specific form of Jewish identity, Franco-Judaism, that took shape in the nineteenth century as a response to the French Revolution.

Writing a Jewish life of Dreyfus also means placing the question of antisemitism front and center. If the affair raised key issues for liberal democracy at a critical moment in world history, it did so because Dreyfus was Jewish. It was not a coincidence that when the French military learned it had a traitor in its ranks, suspicion fell on the one Jew on the General Staff. Although antisemitism was not the sole factor leading to Dreyfus's arrest and conviction, it was the critical one. And it was also critical to why his case divided the French nation. There had been other cases of military espionage, and of wrongful conviction, before Dreyfus, and there have been many since. None turned into an affair. French people cared so deeply about this case—primarily, if not exclusively—because Dreyfus was a Jew.

It was Dreyfus's Jewishness that made the case about more than spying and more than the failures of military justice. As increasing numbers of Jewish immigrants flocked to western democracies in the late nineteenth century, fleeing persecution in Eastern Europe, the so-called Jewish Question—which asked whether Jews belonged in the modern nation-state as full and equal citizens—came to the fore. It was an especially fraught topic of debate in France. France had been the first European country to grant Jews full civil rights, during the French Revolution, but it was also the country where the backlash against

Jewish emancipation was felt most intensely in the late nineteenth century. If you asked observers in 1899, at the height of the Dreyfus Affair, to predict which country was most likely to unleash a genocide against Jews, they would very likely have guessed France.

And yet the Holocaust did not start in France, even if the Vichy government contributed to its implementation. This was largely because the affair defused the time bomb of French antisemitic prejudice, or at least delayed its explosion, by mobilizing much of the French left against right-wing nationalism. The creation of organizations like the Human Rights League during the Dreyfus Affair helped form a bulwark against hatred, as did the courageous stance taken by certain Socialist leaders in defense of the Jewish officer.

Finally, writing a "Jewish life" of Dreyfus means exploring the effect of Dreyfus's life on the lives of Jews around the world. In his humorous story "Dreyfus in Kasrilevke," the Yiddish writer Sholem Aleichem satirizes the way small-town Jews in the Russian empire obsessed over the case. "Paris, they say, seethed like a boiling vat. . . . But the anguish and pain that Kasrilevke underwent, Paris will not experience till Judgment Day," Sholem Aleichem tells us of the reaction to the affair in his fictional Ukrainian shtetl. The effect on Jews was the same in Berlin and New York as in Kasrilevke, and in Chapter 6, I explore how Jewish newspapers in French, English, German, Hebrew, and Yiddish covered the case and understood its implications. The affair offered a kind of mirror in which Jews of all political persuasions saw their hopes and fears reflected, but it also promoted a new model of Jewish solidarity at a moment of great upheaval in Jewish history.

My motivations for focusing on the Jewish aspects of Dreyfus's life might now be clear, but this still leaves open the question of why it is necessary to write a *biography* of Dreyfus in the first place. Although historians have devoted an enormous amount of attention to the affair, relatively few have taken as their primary focus the man at the center of the controversy. There has long been an assumption that since Dreyfus was on Devil's Island while the movement to free him took shape, he played little role in his own affair. The title of one of the classic histories of the case—Marcel Thomas's *L'Affaire sans Dreyfus* (The Affair Without Dreyfus)—encapsulates this approach. There has also been a long-standing assumption that Dreyfus himself was not a very interesting figure—or worse, that he lacked the capacity or inclination to understand the larger issues raised by his case. Léon Blum, an early supporter of the Jewish officer who went on to become France's first Jewish prime minister, famously suggested that if Dreyfus had not been Dreyfus, he might not even have been a Dreyfusard.

In what follows, I return Dreyfus to the center of the story. Drawing on a range of sources, especially his letters and diaries, I present a picture of a very restrained public man that reflects some of the passion that he expressed in private. And I show not only that Dreyfus understood fully what was at stake in the campaign to clear his name, but that he made the campaign possible. Through his heroic resistance to the torture inflicted upon him by the French state—a resistance that required a daily struggle for survival in shockingly brutal conditions over a period of five years—he enabled a gross miscarriage of justice by military and government authorities to come to light. It was only because of his belief in the principles of equality and justice for all, and his willingness to fight for them, that these principles eventually triumphed.[4]

One question that has haunted me, as I researched this book, is what it means to focus on the injustice done to one upper-middle-class (or as the French say, *bourgeois*) white man when the injustice that was constantly being perpetrated upon less privileged people in the nineteenth century often goes unremarked. Lest critics accuse me of anachronism in mentioning this qualm,

I would point out that this was very much a question asked at the time of the affair, when the dominant assumption of the Socialist Party was that the working class should not get involved in the case because a rich military officer like Dreyfus could take care of himself. It was also a question discreetly raised by certain African American supporters of Dreyfus, such as W. E. B. Du Bois and Ida B. Wells-Barnett, who used the case to draw attention to anti-Black racism in the United States.

Without question, the Dreyfus case became an affair because the Dreyfus family possessed the resources to make it one. They spent more than a million francs in their twelve-year struggle for justice.[5] The family members—Dreyfus himself, but also his wife and his brother—were also able to mobilize sufficient *cultural* capital to arouse the sympathy and outrage of Parisian intellectuals. How many victims of similar—or worse—injustice languished in prison, their plight unknown and unremarked because they lacked such resources? How many continue to do so today?

But if Dreyfus's privilege is a fact, it does not negate the value of the struggle undertaken on his behalf. It was thanks to the enormous resources that the Dreyfus family devoted to the case that the ideal of equal justice emerged victorious. It was thanks to their skill and savvy that the forces of right-wing nationalism were at least temporarily held at bay in France and the cause of human rights acquired a new set of institutions to defend it. For this, we are all in their debt.

In 2009, a book appeared with the title *Why the Dreyfus Affair Matters*. The author, Louis Begley, drew a connection between the suffering of the prisoner on Devil's Island and the outrage of Guantanamo, where the United States military continues to hold prisoners for ill-defined reasons of state. Since then, the parallels between the affair and our own moment have only grown more apparent. The life of Dreyfus forces us to consider what it means when the institutions of liberal democracy come under assault and when half a nation commits to believing a lie. The life of Dreyfus also allows us to understand what it takes for truth to triumph against such lies, and how a nation can emerge from political crisis with faith in its institutions intact. As antisemitism and right-wing nationalism stage a comeback in France, the United States, and around the world today, the affair has much to tell us not only about the causes of hatred, but also about the ways it can be resisted. For these and other reasons, the Dreyfus Affair continues to matter, now more than ever.[6]

1

━━━━◆◆◆━━━━

The Soldier

ALFRED DREYFUS was born on October 9, 1859, in the Alsatian town of Mulhouse, on the far northeastern edge of France, near the Swiss border. Jews had lived in the territory of Alsace for more than a thousand years. The name Dreyfus, common among Alsatian Jews, most likely derived from a Roman settlement, Treveris, which later became Trier (Trèves in French), suggesting very ancient roots in the region. Although Alsatian Jews prospered at various points during the Middle Ages, they also experienced periods of brutal violence. In 1349, during the Black Death, Jews were falsely accused of poisoning the wells, and several hundred were massacred in Strasbourg.[1]

A borderland, Alsace passed between different rulers over the course of its history. The province did not become fully French until 1648, when the Treaty of Westphalia brought an end to the Thirty Years War. Technically Jews had been banned from France since 1394, but when Louis XIV took control of

Alsace in the middle of the seventeenth century, he permitted the several thousand Jews in the province to stay. The Sun King likewise made an exception for Alsatian Protestants when he revoked the Edict of Nantes in 1685. Although they were officially tolerated, Alsatian Jews faced numerous legal restrictions until the French Revolution. They were prohibited from living in large towns and cities and prevented from joining guilds or practicing most professions. Aside from a handful of court Jews who made fortunes lending money to nobles and the crown, most Jews in the region scraped by as dealers in grain and livestock, peddlers, and small-scale moneylenders.

Alfred's paternal great-grandfather, Abraham Israel Dreÿfuss, was born in 1749 in Rixheim, a village on the outskirts of Mulhouse with 1,500 Christians and 200 Jews. Alfred's maternal side came from the towns of Ribeauvillé and Bergheim, not far away. Although Jews lived side by side with their gentile neighbors in the small villages of Alsace, they formed a community apart. Governed by a *parnass* (communal leader), they had their own judges to settle business disputes and strictly adhered to Jewish religious laws. Life centered on the synagogue and followed the rhythm of the Jewish calendar—weekly Sabbath rest and frequent holidays. The Jews of Alsace prayed in Hebrew, but mainly spoke Yiddish. Before the French Revolution, few Alsatian Jews were fluent in French, but neither were most of their non-Jewish neighbors, who also spoke a German dialect.[2]

At the time of the French Revolution, the lives of the Jews in the small villages of Alsace resembled those of their fellow Ashkenazic Jews in Central and Eastern Europe. But they were about to diverge. Considered among the most backward populations in France, the Jews of France's eastern provinces began to attract the attention of Enlightenment reformers in the late eighteenth century. In 1787, the Academy of Metz sponsored an essay competition on the theme, "Are there means of making the Jews more useful and happier in France?" Respondents proposed reforms designed to encourage Jewish assimilation—or "regeneration," as they called it. These ranged from banning kosher food to granting full equality. The small communities of Sephardic Jews in the southwest of France, whose ancestors had fled the Spanish and Portuguese Inquisitions and become integrated into French society, were held up as models for their Ashkenazic brethren.

When the Revolution broke out in 1789, the Sephardic Jews of the southwest and the Ashkenazic Jews of Alsace and Lorraine petitioned separately for citizenship. Although many delegates to the revolutionary Constituent Assembly harbored prejudice against Jews, especially against Ashkenazic Jews, they eventually deferred to the principle proclaimed in the *Declaration of the Rights of Man and the Citizen* (1789) that all men were born equal in rights. With two decrees, the first applying to the Sephardim in 1790 and the second to the Ashkenazim in 1791, France made (male) Jews full and equal citizens (women did not gain the right to vote in France until 1944).

It was the first time that a modern European nation had declared the Jews worthy of equality, and it changed the course of Jewish history. Overnight, all the restrictions and prohibitions that had governed Jewish life in France for centuries vanished. There were no longer any legal obstacles preventing French Jews from climbing the economic ladder and participating in the life of the nation. Although Jews in parts of Germany, Italy, and Holland conquered by the French during the Napoleonic Wars also received rights by the early nineteenth century, it would take decades—and more than a century for the millions of Jews in the Russian empire—to attain the freedoms that French Jews gained by the stroke of a pen during the Revolution.

The liberal promise of equality in France was not just an abstract ideal, but a concrete reality. Within a few decades, French

Jews, especially those who had moved to Paris, began to attend prestigious universities, join the liberal professions, and take leading roles in banking and industry. Two Jewish families—the Rothschilds and the Pereires—competed to build the nation's first railroads. In the 1830s, France's most prominent composers—Fromenthal Halévy and Giacomo Meyerbeer—were Jews, as was the star actress of the Comédie Française, Rachel Félix. By the 1840s, three Jews had been elected to the Chamber of Deputies. Although the vast majority of France's Jews had been poor at the time of the Revolution, increasing numbers joined the middle class, the *bourgeoisie*, over the course of the nineteenth century. By the 1850s, when Alfred Dreyfus was born, France's Jews were the best integrated in the world.[3]

The rise of the Dreyfus family typified this rapid social ascent. Alfred's great-grandfather Abraham worked as a kosher butcher in Rixheim. Taking advantage of the relaxation of residency restrictions after the Revolution, he moved with his family to nearby Mulhouse between 1805 and 1808, and died there in 1810. His son Jacob returned to Rixheim temporarily, but by 1821, he was back in Mulhouse, which was becoming the center of France's textile manufacturing industry, the "Manchester of France." Jacob sold cloth, but also acted as a *mohel*, practicing ritual circumcisions for the growing Jewish community of the town. In official documents, he changed his name to Jacques, suggesting a desire—common among upwardly mobile Alsatian Jews—to appear more French. All the members of the Dreyfus family in Alfred's grandparents' generation at the end of the eighteenth century could sign their names, reflecting the high rate of literacy among Alsatian Jews (as high as 80 percent for men). Whereas male members of the family displayed at least the rudiments of a secular education by signing with Latin characters, the women used Hebrew characters.[4]

It was Jacques's son, Raphaël, Alfred's father, who made the family's fortune. Born in 1818, Raphaël started out as a peddler.

By the 1850s, he was serving as a commission agent for one of the many textile mills in Mulhouse, specializing in high-end printed and embroidered fabric. Raphaël opened his own cotton mill in 1862, during the American Civil War, when the sudden unavailability of cotton grown by enslaved people in the American South—which had supplied 90 percent of the raw material for French mills—and the closure of American markets drove many of the more established firms in Mulhouse out of business. This was the moment when the first Jews, who made up a little over 3 percent of the population of Mulhouse, began to penetrate the city's tight-knit coterie of leading industrialists, almost all of whom were Protestant. Although they opened their ranks to Jews, the business elite of Mulhouse remained almost totally closed to Catholics, who made up the majority of the city's working class.[5]

In a photograph showing Raphaël Dreyfus in middle age, he has short-cropped gray hair and very light blue eyes. He does not have a beard and his head is bare, signs that he had left behind his father's traditional religious world even though he continued to practice orthodox Judaism. Although he lacks the elegant bearing that his highly educated children would later display, he wears a frock coat with a starched collar and holds a silk top hat in his lap—a totem of his position as an industrialist. In 1866, Raphaël traded his apartment on the rue du Sauvage, where his twelve children were all born (five died in infancy), for a newly built mansion on the rue de la Sinne, in one of the stately new districts of Mulhouse. The census of 1866 shows that the Dreyfus family employed two servants.[6]

By the time of his death in 1893, Raphaël's fortune approached 800,000 francs, ten times the wealth passed on by his father. This did not make him one of the richest men in Mulhouse, which counted eighty-seven millionaires—the fortune of the Koechlins, a Protestant family, was estimated at 20 million francs in 1875—but it did signify an extraordinarily rapid

Raphaël Dreyfus (Photo © MAHJ/Christophe Fouin)

enrichment, especially considering that the large amounts of money he had already passed on to his children through dowries and other gifts were not included in his estate. In addition to shares in the family textile business, and various properties around Mulhouse, Raphaël's children also inherited seats in the synagogue valued at 2,280 francs.[7]

Raphaël never completely mastered French, but he Gallicized the spelling of his last name from Dreÿfuss to Dreyfus. Whereas many Alsatian Jews gave their children Old Testament first names, only two of the children born to Raphaël and his wife Jeannette (née Libmann), Mathieu and Rachel, bore first names of Hebrew origin. The name Alfred was of more exotic Anglo-Saxon origin and had a certain literary cachet in France, thanks to the Romantic poets Alfred de Musset and Alfred de Vigny.[8]

Raphaël groomed his eldest son, Jacques—named, in keeping with Ashkenazi Jewish custom, after his deceased father—and the second oldest, Léon, to run the family business. But by the 1860s, when it came time to educate his two youngest sons—Mathieu and Alfred—the Dreyfuses possessed the resources to imagine a more ambitious future for them. Taught at first at home by private tutors, and then at the newly founded École professionnelle de Mulhouse, a preparatory school with a French curriculum anchored in modern languages and the exact sciences, Mathieu and Alfred were the first in their family to be fully immersed in French culture.[9]

With a father and older brothers always at the mill, and a mother in poor health after giving birth to Alfred, daily supervision of the household fell largely to the three Dreyfus sisters—Henriette, Louise, and Rachel—especially Henriette, to whom Alfred remained intensely close as an adult. Fine featured with a delicate constitution, Alfred had blond hair, light blue eyes, and a high forehead that would become even more prominent later in life, as his hair receded. He was a smart, curious child, and a bit of a dreamer. According to the reminiscences of a family friend, young Alfred had "exaggerated ideas of honor and justice," which earned him the nickname Don Quixote in his family circle.[10]

The Dreyfuses were observant, if not very devout, Jews. They attended synagogue, but Raphaël did not play a leadership role in the Mulhouse Jewish community. Alfred's sister Henriette participated in some Jewish philanthropic activities, but Raphaël did not leave the Jewish community anything in his will. He was also not among the group of parents of Jewish students at the École professionnelle de Mulhouse who petitioned the mayor to provide Jewish religious instruction in 1868. However, Alfred may have benefited from such instruction along with his regular studies. Because the ruling elite of Mulhouse was dominated by Protestants—who were also a minority and were generally far less antisemitic than the Catholic majority—Mulhouse was unusual among French cities in facilitating supplementary Jewish instruction in public schools.[11]

The Franco-Prussian War of 1870–1871 ruptured Dreyfus's peaceful childhood. Drawn into the conflict by the machinations of the Prussian minister Otto von Bismarck, France experienced a rapid defeat, with 80,000 French troops taken prisoner in just a few months of fighting, including the emperor, Napoleon III. In his memoir, Dreyfus describes experiencing his "first sorrow" as he watched Prussian troops march into Mulhouse from the balcony of the family's house on September 16, 1870.[12] On January 18, 1871, Bismarck proclaimed the creation of the German empire at the royal château of Versailles, a symbolic move calculated to further humiliate the defeated French. As part of the settlement that ended the war, Germany annexed the provinces of Alsace and Lorraine—which had become, thanks to families like the Dreyfuses, the seat of France's industrial economy.

The French experienced the amputation of their eastern provinces as much more than a military and economic blow. It was a trauma that would shape the French national psyche for the next forty years—until France finally recovered Alsace and Lorraine after World War I. Attempting to identify the causes of the defeat in 1871, France subjected itself to a lacerating self-critique. For some—including the novelist Émile Zola, whose novel *La Curée* (The Kill) in 1871 described the sexual perversions of a wealthy family in the decades preceding the debacle—the problem was the decadence of Parisian culture that had emasculated its men and virilized its women. Others blamed the military high command, always fighting the last war and woefully ill-equipped to face Bismarck's modern army. Despite these criticisms, the French army itself took on an almost sacred aura in the decades after 1870, as the country dreamed of exacting vengeance on the Teutonic foe.

Watching in rage as the Prussians entered Mulhouse, the young Alfred Dreyfus developed a passionate hatred for Germany that would fuel his subsequent military vocation. For his parents, the defeat in 1871 had more immediate consequences. Aside from worrying about their son Jacques fighting at the front, they soon faced a difficult decision: should they stay in Alsace to hold on to their business, even if this meant surrendering their French nationality?[13]

All Alsatians faced this difficult choice, but for Jews, the decision was especially difficult. The Dreyfus family had embraced French culture because it was socially advantageous, but they also felt a great loyalty to France for having been the first country to emancipate the Jews. By contrast, the North German Confederation, led by Prussia, had only granted the Jews full civil rights the year before, in 1869. The question of nationality for the Dreyfus family became more urgent when Bismarck declared he would draft young Alsatian men into the German army beginning in 1872. Jacques, the eldest son, was exempt since he had fought for France, but the three younger sons—Léon, Mathieu, and Alfred—faced the prospect of one day having to fight for the enemy.

Some of his fellow Mulhouse mill owners rebuilt their factories across the border in the French city of Belfort to continue to take advantage of French markets, but Raphaël lacked the resources for this maneuver. He therefore decided on a painful compromise. Jacques would remain in Mulhouse and become German, since he was exempt from the German draft, while the rest of the family would take French nationality. As Alfred later put it in his memoir, his father showed no hesitation: "despite

owning important factories, he opted for France, both for himself and for his minor children."[14] In order to declare himself and
his family French, Raphaël needed an official French domicile,
so in May 1872 he traveled to the town of Carpentras, in Pro-
vence, where his eldest daughter Henriette had moved after
marrying Joseph Valabrègue, also from a prominent Jewish textile family. After securing French nationality in October 1872,
Raphaël then moved the family to Basel, Switzerland, which was
close enough to Mulhouse to allow him and his son Léon to remain involved in business affairs. Too sick to make the journey,
his wife Jeannette stayed behind in Mulhouse with Jacques.[15]

Alfred spent the school year in Basel, separated not only
from his mother and oldest brother, but also from his beloved
sister Henriette. To make matters worse, he attended the *Real-
gymnasium* in Basel, where instruction was in German. Though
he spoke the language reasonably well, he struggled academi-
cally. Hungry for the prestige a French education would provide for his youngest children, Raphaël opted for yet more separation: he sent Mathieu and Alfred to Paris to attend boarding
school. Raphaël then moved back to Mulhouse with two of his
older children, Léon and Rachel. (It is unclear what happened
to the other daughter, Louise, but she may have gone to live with
Henriette in Carpentras.) Raphaël requested German citizenship for Rachel, who was still a minor, which gave him and his
wife the right to live in Mulhouse even while retaining French
nationality for themselves.[16]

In 1873, the two youngest Dreyfus boys moved to Paris to
start school: Mathieu attended the Collège Chaptal and Alfred
the Collège Sainte-Barbe. Alfred was miserable in the spartan
atmosphere of the dormitory, which was quite a departure from
the warm and luxurious family home he had known on the rue
de la Sinne. He would later say he "suffered terribly" in his early
days as a boarder, developing a hatred for confinement. He even
went home to Mulhouse for a period and considered stopping

his studies. But he returned to school in Paris—according to a family friend, because he was expelled from Mulhouse as a foreigner by the German authorities. This time, Alfred joined his brother at the Collège Chaptal. Mathieu now lived in his own apartment on the rue Soufflot, near the Panthéon, and the fifteen-year-old Alfred continued to board at the school. Full of ambition but unaccustomed to the customs of the capital, he resembled one of the young provincial protagonists in a novel by Balzac or Stendhal, who comes to Paris to make his fortune.[17]

Naturally reserved, Alfred became a scapegoat for his class-mates. Biographers such as Michael Burns and Vincent Duclert attribute his unpopularity to his fragile health and slight Alsa-tian accent in French. They also speculate it might have been the result of antisemitism. Though the Dreyfus boys were not the only Jews at the Collège Chaptal, they were among the very few. But Alfred experienced this same sense of isolation through-out his life, whenever he left the intimate circle of his family, and his gregarious and handsome older brother does not seem to have suffered in the same way despite also being Jewish and having an accent. Alfred made few close friends. Those around him often tended to interpret his timidity as pride or *hauteur*, which did not help him later in life, especially at his trials, when the public inevitably found him cold and unsympathetic.[18]

In 1875, Mathieu abandoned his studies and served in the French army for a year before returning to Mulhouse to join the family business. This left Alfred alone in Paris. He resolved to stay in school because he now had a new ambition: to enter the École polytechnique, the university focused on engineer-ing, which stood at the pinnacle of the French educational sys-tem. Entrance to the Polytechnique would be a launching pad for a career as a French army officer. Alfred had dreamed of get-ting revenge on Germany ever since he saw Prussian troops enter Mulhouse, and no doubt the sight of his brother in a French uniform reinforced his patriotism. His sister Henriette also helped kindle the fire: "Shouldn't we have at least one officer in our family when the time for vengeance comes?" she reportedly asked Alfred during one of his visits to her home in Carpentras.[19]

Although the German army did not have Jewish officers until World War I, and there were few Jewish officers in the British or American armies before World War II, the situation was different in France. As Derek Penslar explains, military service was compulsory for French Jews during the revolutionary and Napoleonic wars, where it came to be seen as a duty of their newly granted citizenship, and many French Jews embraced a military career in the nineteenth century. France had hundreds of Jewish officers and at least twenty Jewish generals during the Second Empire and Third Republic periods (1851–1940). Many of these officers came from Alsace, where patriotism ran especially high after 1870. Although it did not pay well, a career in the military offered prestige and social capital, which attracted upwardly mobile Jews like the Dreyfus family.[20]

The overrepresentation of Jews in the French army officer corps can also be explained by the increasingly meritocratic nature of that institution. True, many officers still came from traditional backgrounds: the army was long considered a good career option for younger sons of the nobility as well as for the offspring of the bourgeoisie hoping to improve their social standing. These Catholic scions often attended Saint-Cyr, the military academy that had been founded in 1802 by Napoleon. But as the army attempted to modernize in the wake of the Franco-Prussian War, it opened its officer corps to more students from the École polytechnique. Admission to both schools was determined by a competitive entrance examination, but private Jesuit secondary schools had a near monopoly on the preparatory classes necessary to pass the exam for Saint-Cyr. The best preparation for the Polytechnique, on the other hand, could be found at secular public schools, which Jews felt more comfortable attending.

Alfred returned to the Collège Sainte-Barbe, in the Latin Quarter, from 1876 to 1878 to prepare for the entrance exam to Polytechnique. Like most secular public schools, Sainte-Barbe was republican in political orientation, which is to say democratic and left-leaning. Dreyfus met the brother of his future defender, Georges Clemenceau, at Sainte-Barbe and may well have met his other future defender, the Socialist leader Jean Jaurès, at the school as well. Sainte-Barbe had many famous alumni, including Gustave Eiffel, the engineer for the famous tower constructed in 1889. Dreyfus studied hard and managed to pass the entrance exam for the École polytechnique on his first attempt in 1878, although his class rank—182 out of 236— was not quite as high as he might have hoped.[21]

Founded in 1794, during the French Revolution, the École polytechnique had alumni at the highest levels not just of the military, but also in industry, government, and academia. By attending Polytechnique, Alfred kept his options open: if his dream of a military career did not pan out, his engineering expertise would certainly be welcome in the family textile mill or in any other endeavor he chose. The school embodied the technocratic spirit that prevailed in Third Republic France, a period that experienced the vast expansion of France's economy and the modernization of its infrastructure. Like Sainte-Barbe, the school was also republican in political orientation, and by the 1890s, its student body was 3–4 percent Jewish at a time when Jews made up only two-tenths of a percent of the French population. Dreyfus stayed there for two years and managed to improve his academic standing: his class rank at graduation was 128 out of 235.[22]

Upon graduation in 1880, Dreyfus joined the army. Appointed a sub-lieutenant, he attended the artillery training school in Fontainebleau for two years. Once again, his Jewish background may have played a role in his choice, as the artillery corps welcomed Jewish officers more readily than did the cavalry, still an aristocratic bastion. His academic performance continued to improve, and he graduated as number 32 out of 95. A written evaluation by his instructors, which later was cited by his lawyer at trial, was also reasonably favorable: "Good constitution and general health, mildly myopic; good physique; could make a fine officer." If his teachers noticed his Jewishness, they did not see fit to mention it. "There is nothing about him that particularly stands out," they stated in the report.[23]

After spending a year with the 31st artillery division in Le Mans, in the northwest of France, he received a posting with the 1st cavalry division in Paris, a sign that his superiors viewed him favorably. "M[onsieur] Dreyfus is an intelligent officer," wrote his commander in Le Mans in July 1883. "Since his arrival in the corps, he has shown zeal in service and care in maneuvers, but he has a great deal more to do to complete his military instruction." His instructors found fault only with his voice, which they considered monotonous and weak.[24] As Sander Gilman has shown, antisemites often criticized the way Jews spoke in the nineteenth century, faulting not just pronunciation or accent, but the tone of the Jew's voice itself. Dreyfus's "bad intonation"—perhaps the result of trying to hide his slight Alsatian accent—would likewise be held against him at his later trials, when he was never able to summon the proper tone to elicit sympathy from his judges or the public.[25]

Dreyfus continued to receive favorable evaluations throughout his years of training. "He is zealous and conscientious," noted one superior in 1884. Another from 1886 called him "an officer full of fervor, intrepid horseman, well educated, intelligent," and noted that his only defect was his "deplorable intonation." In 1888, he was praised for his "excellent memory and very lively intelligence" and commended for the way he instructed other officers in training.[26]

Dreyfus exemplified many of the qualities that the army sought as it tried to modernize after the defeat of 1871. What he lacked in charisma, he made up for with intelligence and seriousness of purpose. Dreyfus never received a posting to one of the colonial outposts in North Africa or Indochina where he would have had the opportunity to prove his bravery on the battlefield. And unlike the aristocratic graduates of Saint-Cyr, many of whom came from military families, he did not have a powerful protector among the military top brass. A new type of officer, he staked his career on his intellectual capacities. He was a technocrat, a specialist in munitions, which became all the more important as France competed with Germany to develop new weapon systems such as a long-range cannon.

If Dreyfus remained aloof among his fellow officers because of his shy reserve and bookish approach to the art of war, he also stood apart from them because of his income. Government functionaries, including army officers, received only about 2,000 francs a year, barely enough to rent a sparsely furnished apartment and to indulge in the occasional evening at a café or trip to a brothel. Many officers without private means went seriously into debt, especially those who gambled. Thanks to his family's textile business, Dreyfus received between 10,000 and 20,000 francs a year in addition to his regular pay, and he could look forward to a large inheritance, as well as to a dowry if he decided to marry. This substantial fortune enabled him to live in a private apartment on the rue Parmentier, to keep his own horse, and to enjoy the many pleasures of fin-de-siècle Paris—glittering cafés, fine restaurants, and beautiful women. Alfred's tastes ran to older, married demimondaines. His discreet liaisons with a series of such women were later held against him at his trial when prosecutors attempted to depict him as a man of dissolute morals. In reality, he was far more straitlaced than his fellow officers, many of whom seem to have been jealous of his deep pockets.[27]

On several occasions, he made trips back to visit his family in Alsace, which required crossing the border into Germany.

His mother Jeannette died in January 1886, and Dreyfus returned to Mulhouse to say the Jewish prayer for the dead, the
Kaddish, with his family in February 1887, after the year of ritual
mourning ended. These visits across German lines also came to
be held against him at his trial, as the prosecutors attempted to
establish a link between the Jewish officer and the enemy. But
as he completed his training, he continued to enjoy the favor of
his superiors. In 1889, he was promoted to captain and posted
to the artillery school in Bourges, a sign that the army considered his future bright.

After the death of his mother, Dreyfus became more focused and ambitious. It was time to settle down, to think more
seriously about his career and starting a family. He set his sights
on the École supérieure de guerre, the army's elite war college.
Created after the Franco-Prussian War as part of the army's
modernization effort, it provided two years of training in the
latest military tactics and would open the door to the high command. Entrance was based solely on a competitive entrance
exam, and Dreyfus set to work preparing while he taught math-
ematics and mechanical drawing in Bourges. After passing the
written section of the exam for the École supérieure de guerre,
he traveled to Paris to take the oral exam in March and April
1890. On April 20, he learned he had been accepted. The next
day, the thirty-year-old captain got married.

One of the few friends that Dreyfus had made at the École
polytechnique was a fellow Jew, Paul-David Hadamard, who
like Dreyfus became an artillery officer and was appointed to
the rank of captain. In 1889, Hadamard introduced him to his
twenty-year-old cousin Lucie. Lucie Hadamard was Alfred's
physical opposite: tall and robust in constitution, she had a dark
complexion, thick black curly hair that she wore parted in the
center, and dark brown eyes. She had been raised at her family's
country house at Châtou, a wealthy western suburb of Paris favored by Impressionist painters, and educated mainly at home

Lucie Dreyfus (Lorraine Beitler Collection of the Dreyfus Affair,
Kislak Center for Special Collections, Rare Books and Manuscripts,
University of Pennsylvania)

by private tutors. Although she lacked the beauty and sophisti-
cation of the women he frequented as a bachelor (and continued
to frequent for a time after his marriage), Lucie's intelligence
and personal "charm" inspired a "profound affection" in Alfred,
who no doubt was also drawn to her because of her father's
wealth—David Hadamard was one of the capital's leading dia-
mond merchants. For their part, Lucie's parents were sufficiently
impressed by the serious young officer's career prospects to consent to a marriage.[28]

   Although at first glance the Dreyfus and the Hadamard
families seem well matched—both belonged to the Jewish upper
bourgeoisie and both had roots in Alsace-Lorraine—in fact

Alfred had married up. The Dreyfus family was provincial; Alfred was its first member to settle in Paris. In this, he was typical of a generation of European Jews who migrated internally from the outskirts of France, Germany, or the Austrian empire to one of the great capitals (Paris, Berlin, Vienna). By contrast, the Hadamards had already been established in Paris for more than a half century. Lucie's father, David, was born in the capital in 1837 and came from an illustrious family in Metz. Lucie's great-grandmother Rebecca Hadamard (née Lambert) had succeeded in obtaining permission during the Reign of Terror to bake matzoh for Passover despite laws against the practice of religion, and protested the desecration of the Jewish cemetery in Metz, leading to the punishment of the vandals. Remembered as a heroine by the Jewish community, she provided a model for Lucie in her later struggles to clear her husband's name.[29]

More recently, several members of the Hadamard family had attended the École polytechnique. One cousin was the philosopher Lucien Lévy-Bruhl and another was the mathematician Jacques Hadamard. Lucie's mother Louise (née Hatzfeld) was also the daughter of a graduate of Polytechnique and one of her relatives, the linguist Adolphe Hatzfeld, had authored an important French dictionary. Whereas Alfred's father had earned the family fortune himself, Lucie's family's wealth stretched back several generations. More significantly, if Alfred and his brother Mathieu were the first members of the Dreyfus family to feel at home in French culture, and Alfred was the first to aspire to a career outside of trade, many members of Lucie's family were accomplished professionals and intellectuals. They had reached a higher level of social integration than the Dreyfuses.[30]

I use the term *integration* rather than *assimilation* to refer to the way that families like the Dreyfuses and the Hadamards adapted themselves to French culture. This is an important distinction, and it represents a departure from the way a previous generation of scholars thought about nineteenth-century French

Jews. In her influential account of the Dreyfus Affair in *The Origins of Totalitarianism*, the German Jewish political philosopher Hannah Arendt describes how "The Dreyfus family belonged to that section of French Jewry which sought to assimilate by adopting its own brand of antisemitism."[31] Arendt is referring to the attempt by Jews like Dreyfus to ape the aristocracy by pursuing careers in the military. She repeatedly uses the term "assimilation" to connote the surrender of Jewish identity and affiliation in the rush to become French: "When the Dreyfus Affair broke out to warn them that their security was menaced, they were deep in the process of a disintegrating assimilation," Arendt says of the French Jews.[32] Similarly, the historian Michael Marrus, who titles his account of the French Jewish community at the time of the Dreyfus Affair *The Politics of Assimilation*, defines assimilation as "the process by which individuals of Jewish background assumed an identity which is essentially French." And although Marrus acknowledges that "assimilation has many different forms and degrees," his book is essentially an indictment of the way the French Jews were unprepared to cope with the outbreak of antisemitism during the Dreyfus Affair because they had surrendered their Jewish identity.[33]

But did families like the Dreyfuses and the Hadamards really surrender their Jewish identity as they became French? Had their bonds with other Jews really "disintegrated" to the extent that they left Judaism behind or even became antisemitic, as Arendt alleges? It is true that some Jews in nineteenth-century France did make this leap. The press baron Arthur Meyer, who published the conservative daily *Le Gaulois*, converted to Catholicism and became a right-wing nationalist—as well as an ardent anti-Dreyfusard. But the number of Jews who followed this path was vanishingly small.

The great majority of French Jews, including the Dreyfus and Hadamard families, remained Jewish even as they attended the most prestigious French schools, wrote dictionaries of the

French language, or joined the French army. The ideology of Franco-Judaism that took shape over the course of the nineteenth century did not view the process of becoming French as a zero-sum game for Jews. Indeed, for the generations of Jews who integrated into French culture in the nineteenth century, Frenchness and Jewishness went hand in hand.

This was because the France they loved and yearned to be part of was the France of the Revolution, the France that had declared its fidelity to universalist values by granting the Jews full civil rights. As Jews, they therefore felt doubly French, since it was their emancipation that had helped define the new kind of nation that France had become. The French Revolution was "our second law of Sinai," according to Isidore Cahen, the editor of the French Jewish newspaper *Les Archives israélites.*[34] "And why should we not love France?" asked Rabbi Moïse Schuhl of Saint-Étienne in a sermon reprinted in the rival newspaper, *L'Univers israélite.* "It was France that was the first to decree that it did not take religious distinctions into account, that it considered the Israelites as its children, just like all other French people. If Israelites now enjoy political rights in most other civilized countries, it is to France, it is to the principles of the French Revolution, that they owe them."[35]

Jewish religious practice underwent change in nineteenth-century France. Unlike in Germany or the United States, there were no reform synagogues in France, so many French Jews simply stopped following religious laws while continuing to pray—on major holidays—in the orthodox synagogue. The men of the Dreyfus and Hadamard families may not have worn beards or covered their heads, but they continued to perform certain rituals, such as saying the Kaddish prayer for the dead. In one of her first letters to her husband after his arrest, dated December 30, 1894, Lucie writes, "Tonight is the anniversary of your father's death, we will all go to temple."[36] The Dreyfus Collection in the Musée d'art et d'histoire du Judaïsme in Paris contains *yahrzeit* calendars, printed in Hebrew and French, which allowed Alfred to commemorate the dates of his parents' deaths according to the Hebrew lunar calendar. There is a similar one in German, printed in Prague, for Lucie's parents. The archive also contains an ivory-covered Hebrew prayer book owned by Lucie, engraved with her initials, and inscribed inside with the dates (according to both the Gregorian and Hebrew calendars) of her grandparents' and great-grandparents' deaths. The fact that not only did Alfred and Lucie possess these objects but that they preserved them as family relics—the objects were donated to the museum by their descendants—show that the Jewish religion retained a place of importance in their lives, even if they may not have practiced it on a daily basis.[37]

It is important to note that Alfred Dreyfus rarely mentions God in his writings and never refers to his Jewish faith. He was a rationalist and a skeptic, unlike Lucie, who was more of a believer, although she also rarely mentioned religion in the letters she wrote to her husband during his imprisonment and often used Christian terms, such as "calvary," to describe their plight.[38] But this does not mean that Judaism as a religion or culture had ceased to play a role in their lives. If Alfred and Lucie did not speak of their Jewishness in writings that they intended for public consumption—and they knew that their letters would be read by prison authorities and perhaps eventually published— it was likely because they believed it was a private matter. Unlike their pre-revolutionary ancestors, whose Jewishness defined every aspect of their lives, nineteenth-century French Jews like the Dreyfuses considered Judaism a religion only. To signal this change, they referred to themselves as *Israélites*, which they considered a more distinguished term than *Juif* or Jew. They were French men and women of the Mosaic persuasion, similar in every respect to their fellow French men and women except when it came time to worship. Jewishness played an important part in their lives, but a discreet one.

It is also important to note that even if French Jews sought
to resemble their gentile compatriots in their customs and hab-
its, from their choice of profession to their style of dress, they
nevertheless retained all the characteristics of a distinct subculture. As was typical of nineteenth-century French Jews, who
had very low rates of conversion and intermarriage, every single one of Alfred Dreyfus's siblings married a Jew. And all were
married in the synagogue except Mathieu, whose wife came
from a family of Jewish nonbelievers. Alfred and Lucie celebrated their own nuptials in the Grand Synagogue of Paris, on
the rue de la Victoire, which had opened to the public in 1875.
The ceremony was performed by Zadoc Kahn, the Chief Rabbi
of France, who was a friend of the Hadamard family. Both of
Alfred and Lucie's two children—Pierre and Jeanne—also married Jews, as did almost all members of the Dreyfus and Hadamard families at least through World War II.[39] Although Alfred did not take part in communal activities, both Lucie and
Pierre assumed leadership roles in Jewish charitable institutions.
As was typical of their class and milieu, most of their friends
and associates were other highly acculturated Jews.[40]

Contrary, then, to what Arendt asserts, the Dreyfuses were
not "assimilated" Jews, if by assimilated we mean Jews who had
ceased to feel a distinct Jewish identity or a connection to other
Jews. Dreyfus never sought to hide his Jewishness, and unlike
some of his fellow Jewish officers, he was not ashamed of it, as
an examining magistrate at his trial noted. He was certainly not
an "antisemite" as Arendt bizarrely alleges. But one wonders
if some of his reluctance to discuss his Jewishness in public
may have resulted from his effort to keep this aspect of himself
walled off from public view.[41]

One of the tragedies of Dreyfus's life was his inability to
bridge the gap between his public and private selves. He was
never comfortable with strangers, and his apparent aloofness
was later held against him at his trials and remarked upon by

those who observed him in prison, where it was frequently in-
terpreted as a sign of his guilt. Even sympathetic historians have
tended to characterize Dreyfus as unlikable. And yet, his private writings—his diary and especially his letters to his wife—
express a great deal of emotion and reveal a sensitive, thoughtful
nature. Perhaps some of what observers perceived as the rigid-
ity of his bearing and the uncommunicativeness of his public
persona resulted from the strain of conforming to a certain ideal
that he thought was expected of him as an Israelite officer in
the French army.[42]

At the same time, Dreyfus believed that his Jewish background should not pose an obstacle to his advancement in the
military, and he was not afraid to stand up for himself as a Jew.
This became clear during his time at the École de guerre, where
competition was fierce to be among the top twelve members of
the graduating class who would automatically receive a coveted
internship on the General Staff (État-major général), the inner
sanctum of the French military, referred to colloquially as the
arche-sainte, the "Holy of Holies." In his final year, one of Dreyfus's examiners, General Pierre de Bonnefond, an antisemite who
had declared openly that he did not want a Jew on the General
Staff, awarded Dreyfus a top grade (19/20) for technical accomplishment, but a zero for the so-called côte d'amour, a subjective grade for character. The other Jewish student in the class
received a similarly low character grade. At his trial at Rennes
in 1899, Dreyfus recounted the incident: "My comrade was very
upset; I was also very upset and found it contemptible, so he asked
me what could be done. Since I ranked higher (he was a lieutenant and I was a captain), I told him that the only thing we could
do was to file a complaint with our superiors." Dreyfus brought
the matter to the head of the school, General Jules Abel Leb-
elin de Dionne. Without changing the grade, the general explained that it had very little significance. In Dreyfus's case,
instead of graduating fourth or fifth in his class, he graduated in

ninth place, which still entitled him to an internship on the General Staff. Dreyfus considered the matter closed.[43]

This incident reveals the extent to which Dreyfus believed in the ideals of French universalism, its promise to treat all citizens in an equal manner. It also reveals an almost touching—some would say naïve—confidence in the willingness of the French military command to enforce those ideals. Dreyfus pursued a similar strategy after his conviction for treason, when he fired off letter after letter to his superiors, even to the president of the Republic, trusting that once they understood the injustice that had been done to him, they would rectify it.

Was this confidence—and by extension the confidence of all French Jews in the nation that had made them citizens—misplaced? Was the entire premise of Franco-Judaism built on shaky ground? The outpouring of antisemitism during the Dreyfus Affair, and certainly the mass deportation of French Jews during World War II, might make us think so. But it is important to avoid evaluating the attitudes of Jews in the nineteenth century through the lens of hindsight. If the affair took place in France rather than, say, in Germany or Russia, or for that matter the United States, it was in part because France had welcomed Jews into the military and allowed them to rise in the military ranks. A Jew like Dreyfus would simply not have gotten as far as he did, and therefore would not have become a target, in these other countries. Even though he experienced a certain degree of antisemitism during the early days of his military career, Dreyfus had every reason to trust a system that had allowed a Jew like him to succeed.

2

The Arrest

DREYFUS BEGAN HIS INTERNSHIP on the General Staff in January 1893, hoping that it would lead to a permanent position. The General Staff had four *bureaux*, or sections, and Dreyfus rotated through them all over the course of his two-year training period, mastering the finer points of modern military strategy, such as the use of rail supply lines and the ins and outs of the latest German weapon systems. At the Third Bureau, which oversaw troop maneuvers, he worked under Commandant Georges Picquart, a rising star in the officer corps, who had been his teacher.

Dreyfus impressed his superiors with his great curiosity—a trait that would later strike them as suspicious. At the time, however, he received mostly high marks. "His beginnings on the army's General Staff have been good," wrote Major General Arthur Gonse, the second-in-command, in his evaluation of Dreyfus at the end of his first year. "Captain Dreyfus is driven by the desire to do well and to succeed. Officer with a future."[1]

Dreyfus had a bright future at home as well. He lived in a large apartment on the avenue du Trocadéro, in the sixteenth arrondissement of Paris. Thanks to Lucie's dowry as well as the revenue he received from the family business, the newlyweds enjoyed an annual income of 40,000 francs a year, roughly twenty times the amount the army paid its officers, and their fortune grew still greater after Alfred's father's death in 1893. This meant that they could afford servants, horses, and other luxuries. More significantly, though, Dreyfus had a family he loved and who adored him in return. In addition to Lucie and his devoted siblings in Mulhouse and Carpentras, he now had a son, Pierre, born in 1891, and daughter, Jeanne, born in 1893. A friend later remarked that Dreyfus had never seemed so happy as in the weeks before his arrest.[2]

He did not give a second thought to the summons that arrived at his home on Saturday, October 15, 1894, requesting that he appear for an inspection at the ministry of war on Monday morning at 9 A.M. The order to dress in civilian clothes might have struck him as odd, but he had no reason to believe anything could be wrong as he made his way on foot across the river to the Left Bank. Arriving early at the ministry, he waited for a few minutes in the courtyard on the rue Saint-Dominique. It was Picquart who escorted him to the office of the chief of the General Staff, General Raoul de Boisdeffre. Dreyfus later described feeling surprise at not seeing any of his fellow interns. Instead, he was greeted by four unknown men, three of whom wore civilian clothes. The one officer in uniform, Commandant Armand du Paty de Clam, asked him to take dictation. Unknown to Dreyfus, an intelligence officer—Commandant Hubert-Joseph Henry—hid behind the curtains, observing his every gesture.[3]

An aristocratic graduate of Saint-Cyr, Du Paty de Clam resembled a bird of prey, with long legs, a thin body, small dark eyes, and a handlebar moustache that twisted up at the corners in a parody of a smile. After instructing Dreyfus to take a seat, he said that he needed to write a letter for General de Boisdeffre to sign but that he had hurt his hand. He then furnished Dreyfus with paper and pen and proceeded to dictate an oddly disjointed missive that featured a hydraulic cannon, Madagascar, and other seemingly unconnected words and bits of information. Dreyfus had no inkling that the intelligence services wanted to collect a specimen of his handwriting to compare with a letter they had recently discovered offering to sell French military secrets to Germany.

Halfway through the dictation, Du Paty de Clam declared, "You are trembling!" Dreyfus, who was not trembling, responded that his fingers were perhaps still a bit cold from his walk over and continued writing. A few moments later, Du Paty de Clam interrupted himself again: "Pay attention. This is very serious!" Then, once he had finished dictating, he took the paper, placed his hand on Dreyfus's shoulder, and theatrically proclaimed, "In the name of the law, I arrest you; you are accused of the crime of high treason."[4]

A fierce patriot, Dreyfus had devoted his career to serving France. He would sooner have laid down his life for the army than betray it. He assumed that an error had been made. How could he of all people be accused of such a monstrous crime? But if he was flabbergasted at the accusation, it was because his intense patriotism kept him from acknowledging the reality of his situation. For nearly a decade, a powerful force had been taking shape in France, a force opposed to his rise through the military ranks and especially to his entry onto the General Staff. That force was antisemitism.

France has always posed a conundrum for scholars of antisemitism: the European country that showed the most openness to Jews was also the country where modern antisemitism first took shape. However, what seems like a paradox is not one; antisemitism developed in direct reaction to that openness. It was the new visibility of Jews in high-profile arenas in France— the republican state apparatus, the arts, and especially banking— in the late nineteenth century that made them targets both for xenophobic nationalists on the right and for a certain strain of Socialists on the left.

By the 1880s, France was increasingly divided between two competing visions of its past and future. One was progress-oriented. It welcomed the changes brought about by the French Revolution—the political, economic, and social liberalism that had triumphed by the end of the nineteenth century. The other was disgruntled and nostalgic. It yearned for a return to the old feudal order and for a society rooted in religious values. This reactionary faction found adherents principally among the segments of society that had been left behind by capitalist modernity—impoverished aristocrats, fundamentalist Catholics, insecure shopkeepers, and some segments of the rural peasantry.[5]

All these groups had been conditioned to hate Jews by centuries of prejudice, rooted in Christian teaching and exacerbated by hostility toward Jewish economic practices during the medieval and early modern periods, when moneylending was one of the few professions Jews were allowed to practice. Now, as modernity took hold, attitudes toward Jews became the dividing line between the two Frances. Whereas the modernizers welcomed Jews or were at least indifferent to them, the reactionaries expressed their frustration as antisemitism. Put in the terms of the historian Shulamit Volkov, antisemitism came to serve as a "cultural code" or shorthand expressing opposition to all the changes associated with modernity, including parliamentary democracy, finance capitalism, and secularization. This antisemitic "cultural code" first began to take shape in the decades immediately after the French Revolution but reached a pinnacle at the end of the nineteenth century. During the Drey-fus Affair, it became a battle line in an ideological civil war.[6]

One of the first to sense the potential of antisemitism to galvanize the disaffected segments of French society was Éd-ouard Drumont. From a modest family of artisans, Drumont worked as a journalist, specializing in nostalgic works such as *Mon vieux Paris* (My Old Paris, 1879), in which he lamented the transformation of the French capital into a modern metropolis. Grasping for topics that might attract a wider readership, he eventually found in antisemitism the door to a vast stockroom of resentment.

His magnum opus *La France juive* (Jewish France) in 1886 began with the preposterous assertion that "The Jew alone prof-ited from the French Revolution."[7] Drumont's paranoid screed proceeded to detail how a horde of Semitic invaders had man-aged, in less than a hundred years since their emancipation, to seize control of the nation's wealth, reducing "real" Frenchmen like himself to the status of feudal serfs. Drumont's formula proved attractive because it attributed everything that was bad about the modern world to the nefarious plotting of a small but potent cabal of Jews. Combining the Socialist antipathy toward Jewish bankers with the right-wing hostility of ultraroyalists and fundamentalist Catholics, Drumont stirred in a dose of the latest racial theorizing to produce a toxic synthesis of all the various forms of antisemitism then in circulation. Hitler would later take it as a model.

A master of pseudoscientific discourse, Drumont made de-monstrably false claims and backed up his lies with inscrutable charts and tables, carefully footnoted to make them seem legiti-mate. Much of the book consisted of lists of Jewish bankers and politicians, many of whom—like Prime Minister Léon Gam-betta—he declared to be Jewish even though they were not.[8] Like all mythical demons, Drumont's Jews were at once all-powerful and the embodiment of every negative quality imaginable, both physical and moral. Using terms borrowed from the linguist Ernest Renan, who was not an antisemite, Drumont cast the Jews not just as a religious minority, but as a distinct "Semitic" race that was biologically inferior to the "Aryan" majority yet able to destroy it through rapacious cunning. For Drumont, the Jewish takeover of France was a war that France had already lost. The public devoured his book: it went through multiple editions, selling 65,000 copies in the first year and more than 100,000 by 1914, an enormous success for Flammarion, the publisher.[9]

La France juive ushered in a period of intense antisemitism in France. Indeed, hatred of Jews was so pervasive in the French literary sphere that it infiltrated every form of discourse, from novels to theater to newspapers. In 1892, Drumont capitalized on his book's success by creating a daily newspaper dedicated to attacking Jews. In an ironic nod to the liberal values he despised, Drumont titled it *La Libre parole* (Free Speech), and by 1894 the illustrated newspaper had a circulation of 200,000. This success came despite fierce competition from other antisemitic publications: *La Croix*, published by the Catholic Assumptionist order, tried to outmaneuver Drumont by declaring itself "France's most anti-Jewish newspaper."[10]

Although it may seem difficult to believe that multiple daily newspapers could fill their pages with invective directed against such a tiny segment of the French population (two-tenths of one percent, 80,000 out of 40 million in metropolitan France), their hate was fueled by a series of scandals, including the Panama Affair, which implicated prominent politicians in a bribery and corruption scheme to finance the canal. Several Jewish bankers were implicated in the scandal, including Jacques de Reinach, who leaked crucial details about the scheme to Drumont, hoping to convince the journalist to keep his own name out of *La Libre parole*. But his plan backfired: Drumont's newspaper gained in importance and Reinach committed suicide.[11]

A typical issue of *La Libre parole* might juxtapose "humorous" antisemitic poems and popular songs alongside conspiratorial denunciations of French politicians and public figures, featuring the kind of pseudo-reporting that Drumont had employed in *La France juive*. Images were critical to its success. The artists for *La Libre parole* perfected a visual vocabulary for representing Jewish monstrosity—hooked noses, flaring ears, grasping fingers, and pockets stuffed with banknotes. One cover showed such a creature dashing atop the stock exchanges of Berlin and Paris carrying a bag of money. Another showed a grotesque "Semite" clutching a globe with the legend "Their Homeland" (*Leur patrie*) to underscore the theme of Jewish cosmopolitanism.

Drumont devoted special attention to Jews in the French military. Beginning on May 23, 1892, two months after its founding and just as Dreyfus completed his time at the École de guerre, *La Libre parole* launched a series of articles titled "Jews in the Army." According to the author, Paul de Lamase (likely a pseudonym), the military had managed to resist the Semitic "invasion" longer than other French institutions, thanks to its ingrained conservatism, but this began to give way after 1870. "Already masters of finance, of administration, dictating the decisions of tribunals, they [the Jews] will soon be the definitive masters of France the day when they command the army," the first article warned. "Rothschild will then have himself sent the mobilization plans—and we know with what intent!"[12] Not satisfied with slandering Jewish officers in general—whom he derisively lumped together as "The Cahens, the Dreyfuses," using two of the most common French Jewish names—Lamase called out specific Jews, whom he accused of having pulled strings to grab plum positions in Paris, while real French soldiers got sent off to get themselves killed in dangerous colonial outposts like Tunisia and Algeria.[13] As one contemporary observer put it, these articles "persuaded a part of the public and a part of the army that Jewish officers were perpetual candidates for treason."[14]

Cover of *La Libre Parole*, October 28, 1893 (Lorraine Beitler Collection of the Dreyfus Affair, Kislak Center for Special Collections, Rare Books and Manuscripts, University of Pennsylvania)

Although critics such as Arendt and Marrus have accused
fin-de-siècle French Jews of minimizing the threat of antisemitism and responding to assaults "passively," this was not actually the case.[15] Zadoc Kahn, who as Chief Rabbi of France acted
as a kind of official spokesman for the community, responded
to provocations in *La Libre parole* and *La Croix* with tireless letters to the editors of more sympathetic newspapers. The Rothschilds discreetly funded some of these publications. In 1893,
with Rothschild backing, a Jewish journalist named Isidore Singer
launched a biweekly newspaper with the explicit goal of countering Drumont and affirming the loyalty of Jews to France.
He titled his paper *La Vraie parole* (True Speech) and set as its
motto: "With God, for Humanity, for the Fatherland, and for
Justice." Although some leading Jewish intellectuals wrote for it,
La Vraie parole failed to find an audience and could not compete
with the two other Jewish weekly newspapers—*Les Archives israélites* and *L'Univers israélite*. It folded at the end of 1894, just
as Dreyfus was accused of treason.[16]

Other Jews took up actual arms against the antisemites. Unlike in Germany, where Jews were considered *nichtsatisfaktions-
fähig*, or unworthy of fighting, French Jews actively participated
in the culture of dueling, which remained an essential means
of settling disputes among gentlemen when honor was at stake.
After the publication of the series of articles attacking Jews in
the army in *La Libre parole*, a French Jewish officer named André
Crémieu-Foa—one of the few Jews in the cavalry—published a
letter in the press challenging Drumont to a duel on behalf of
the "three hundred active army officers who belong to the Jewish religion."[17] The combat (with swords) took place on June 1,
1892, and was so violent that a doctor stopped it after both men
had been injured. One of Crémieu-Foa's seconds in the duel was
none other than Commandant Ferdinand Walsin Esterhazy, the
man who committed the act of treason for which Dreyfus later
ended up being condemned, but who was happy to lend a hand

to his Jewish comrades when the occasion arose, especially since it justified his subsequent attempts to ask the Rothschilds and other prominent Jews for money.

This combat did not settle the matter. One of Drumont's seconds, the marquis de Morès, a notorious adventurer and anti-semite, challenged Crémieu-Foa to a duel, which ended without bloodshed. Morès then challenged another Jewish officer, Armand Mayer, who had also acted as Crémieu-Foa's second. This duel took place on June 23, 1892. Alsatian and a graduate of Polytechnique like Dreyfus, Mayer was mortally wounded by Morès's sword. His death struck a chord not just among Jews but among all those who were outraged by Drumont's anti-semitic attacks: more than 20,000 people expressed their solidarity with the Jewish community by attending Mayer's funeral, where they heard Zadoc Kahn recite the Kaddish prayer.

Dreyfus was away from Paris and did not attend the funeral of his classmate. And he made no reference to antisemitism in any of his published writings. His son Pierre explains in the preface to his father's *Souvenirs* (Recollections) that Dreyfus considered antisemitism a "cloud" hanging over the country, but "did not attach too great an importance to it," at least before his arrest.[18]

After his arrest, however, Dreyfus understood himself to be a victim of antisemitism. During the prolonged period of investigation before the trial, when Dreyfus found himself subjected to a Kafkaesque series of interrogations, Ferdinand Forzinetti, the sympathetic commander of the Cherche-Midi Prison, reported him saying, "My only crime is being born a Jew."[19] Joseph Reinach, the first historian of the Dreyfus Affair and nephew of Jacques de Reinach, who had been compromised in the Panama scandal, claims that Dreyfus repeated this statement on multiple occasions during the ordeal that followed.[20] And Dreyfus's sister Rachel Schil echoed this same language in a letter she wrote to the governor-general of Paris on December 28, 1894: "Think of the martyrdom of this man whose only crime is being Jewish."[21] The fact that Dreyfus did not make the link to antisemitism in any of his published writing about the affair reveals that just as he chose to remain discreet about his religious beliefs, he considered his feelings about antisemitism to be a private matter. Perhaps, also, he thought it wiser not to dignify antisemitism by referring to it in print.

In fact, before his arrest, Dreyfus had experienced relatively little open antisemitism in the army, except for when he received the low grade from the antisemitic instructor at the École de guerre. His experience was not unique: despite the rising tide of antisemitism in the 1880s, the French military remained welcoming to Jews until the Dreyfus Affair soured the atmosphere. Of the thousands of evaluations of French Jewish officers reviewed by Derek Penslar for his study of Jews in the military, almost none displayed overt or even implied antisemitism before the affair. Many were glowing. The evaluation of Armand Mayer, a year before his tragic death at the hands of the marquis de Morès, described him as intelligent, tactful, and an excellent horseman: "a remarkable officer from all points of view." An earlier evaluation described him as an "Israelite of tall stature and very blond, correct and military bearing," suggesting that the evaluator was both aware of Mayer's Jewish background and intent on showing that Mayer did not conform to antisemitic stereotypes. Dreyfus himself received almost uniformly positive reviews during his military training, which perhaps explains why he felt emboldened to complain about his one unfairly negative assessment.[22]

But even though the French military as a whole welcomed Jews, the General Staff was a different matter. Many historians of the affair have stated that Dreyfus was the first Jew on the General Staff. This is not, strictly speaking, true. The General Staff went through many iterations over the course of the nineteenth century. For most of the century, its permanent membership included all of the army's generals, so many Jews were on it. A Jewish colonel named Abraham Samuel figured as one of the General Staff's highest administrative officers in the early 1880s. Between 1888 and 1890, however, the General Staff underwent restructuring. Under the leadership of General Joseph de Miribel, it began to seek out the best and brightest officers in the army. It was thanks to this new meritocratic system that the General Staff began to recruit automatically the top twelve graduates of the École de guerre, which is how Dreyfus became an intern. And Dreyfus was in fact the first Jew to have joined the newly reconstituted General Staff, the "Holy of Holies."[23]

Miribel's meritocratic reforms, which were likely to result in many more Jews joining the General Staff in years to come, generated a backlash. As Duclert has argued, some of Dreyfus's superiors and fellow trainees resented him not because he was a Jew, but because he represented a new type of officer—intellectual, analytical, and a Polytechnique graduate. Dreyfus was the very incarnation of the new modernizing trend. When his examiners faulted him for lacking a commanding voice and for displaying too much zeal in his effort to understand technical aspects of warfare, they were suggesting that he did not conform to traditional notions of what a military officer should be. Was this disdain for Dreyfus as a modernizer also tinged with antisemitism? Yes, in the sense that though not all the modernizers were Jewish, all the Jews were modernizers or perceived as such. Opposition to modernization and opposition to Jews both stemmed from the same reactionary impulse in the army and French society at large. When General de Bonnefond said he didn't want a Jew on the General Staff, he meant not just an officer who practiced Judaism or belonged to the Jewish "race," but an officer who was going to change the military's culture.[24]

Whether he realized it or not, Dreyfus's Jewish background became a major obstacle to his career advancement once he began his internship on the General Staff. When he graduated from the École de guerre, Lieutenant Colonel Jean Sandherr, the head of the Statistical Section (Intelligence) of the General Staff, also a native of Alsace, begged General de Miribel not to let a Jew into the "Holy of Holies." Picquart, who shared the anti-semitic prejudices prevalent among Catholic graduates of Saint-Cyr, arranged for Dreyfus to begin his internship in the section dedicated to troop maneuvers, where he would not have access to classified information. He placed Dreyfus under the direct command of Major Armand Mercier-Milon, known to be free from antisemitism, so it is possible that Picquart also thought he was doing Dreyfus a favor. But, according to Reinach, "anti-semitism, in this clericalist milieu, overheated by reading the murderous prose of Drumont, did not cease to haunt him [Drey-fus] for an instant."[25] Duclert wagers that without powerful pro-tectors, family connections, or the leadership qualities valued by the traditionalists, Dreyfus would have been denied a per-manent position on the General Staff despite his technical bril-liance even had he never been charged with treason. Some of his superiors were determined to block his path.[26]

But does this mean he was accused of treason because he was Jewish? That is one of the central questions of the affair, and it has given rise to debate among historians. Of course, we can never know the real motivations of Dreyfus's accusers with certainty. They themselves might not have known why they sus-pected, or pretended to suspect, the lone Jewish officer on the General Staff once evidence came to light that an officer in the army had committed treason. But the events leading up to the arrest suggest that Dreyfus's Jewishness played a major role in the case.

These events began with the discovery of the document known as the *bordereau*—meaning "note" or "memorandum"—in late September 1894. The document, ripped in several pieces, came into the possession of the French counterintelligence ser-vice via the so-called "ordinary track." A cleaning woman in the

German embassy, Marie Bastian, would collect the trash in the office of the German military attaché Maximilien von Schwarz-koppen and deliver it to her contact at the Statistical Section, Commandant Henry, whose office was on the same street, the rue de Lille. Apparently, the Germans did not worry about Bastian disposing of confidential documents because they knew her to be illiterate. After easily assembling the six torn pieces, Henry realized he had found proof that someone in the French army was selling secrets to the Germans. The bordereau offered to supply information concerning the hydraulic brake of the 120-millimeter cannon, as well as information about troop maneuvers, a firing manual for the field artillery, a report concerning the modification of artillery formations, and another report concerning Madagascar.

Recognizing the significance of his discovery, Henry showed the bordereau to his colleagues in the Statistical Section, Jules Lauth and Félix Gribelin, who in turn showed it to Lieutenant Colonel Sandherr, the officer in charge. The information offered in the bordereau was not terribly important, and the discovery might not have turned into an affair had General Auguste Mercier not taken an interest in the case. A graduate of the École polytechnique, Mercier was considered a modernizer, and his appointment as minister of war in May 1894 had angered the far right. Drumont repeatedly attacked him in *La Libre parole* for being allied with Jews. Mercier believed that by catching the spy he could prove his own efficacy, and he therefore put pressure on his underlings to unmask the bordereau's author as quickly as possible.[27]

Soon the officers of the Statistical Section developed a theory that the spy had to be an intern on the General Staff because only someone who moved between divisions would have had access to such disparate information. Furthermore, given the nature of the information on munitions, they speculated that the spy was probably an artillery officer. This narrowed down the list of possible culprits, several of whom one of the officers, Colonel Pierre Fabre, knew personally since he supervised one of the sections of the General Staff that the interns had rotated through. He immediately suspected Dreyfus, having given him the one mediocre evaluation he received during his internship. "Incomplete officer, very intelligent and very gifted, but pretentious and not meeting expectations in terms of character, conscience, and the means of fulfilling the conditions necessary for being employed on the General Staff of the Army," Fabre had written.[28]

On October 6, Fabre and Lieutenant Colonel Albert d'Aboville compared the handwriting of the bordereau to that of Dreyfus and believed it matched. Similarities did exist. However, there were also major differences, and the expert graphologists who testified at Dreyfus's trial were divided in their conclusions. One of them, the eccentric Alphonse Bertillon, well known for his use of photography to identify and classify criminals, advanced the theory that Dreyfus had attempted to disguise his own handwriting in the bordereau, the outlandish "self-forgery" hypothesis. That the counterespionage officers of the Statistical Section were willing to believe such a theory suggests that they were swayed by something other than the facts of the case.[29]

Reinach assumes it was antisemitism: if there hadn't been a Jew among the interns on the General Staff, he reasons, the counterespionage team would have quickly realized that the spy could not actually have been an artillery officer because he spoke in such uncertain terms about artillery. They also would have realized that the spy could not have been an intern on the General Staff because the author of the bordereau said he was going on maneuvers at a time and place that would have been impossible for the interns of the General Staff to do. "But the idea of the Jew took hold, seized them, dominated them," Reinach writes of the officers, including Sandherr and Mercier, who accused

Dreyfus.[30] They wanted Dreyfus to be guilty because he was a Jew, so they convinced themselves that the evidence pointed in that direction. In the preface to Dreyfus's *Souvenirs*, his son Pierre likewise assumes that suspicion fell on his father because he was "the only Jew" on the General Staff.[31]

Other scholars believe that Reinach exaggerated the importance of Dreyfus's Jewishness. According to Duclert, it is simply not correct that the members of the high command were all obsessive antisemites. They were antisemitic, Duclert acknowledges, but not to the extent that they would have blamed Dreyfus simply because he was a Jew. What mattered more to the high command was that Dreyfus was considered a modernizer. The conservative officers on the General Staff never wanted him there to begin with and were determined to keep him from obtaining a permanent position. That is why he fell so quickly under suspicion. But as we have seen, the conservatives did not really distinguish between Jews and modernizers. They were essentially the same thing: non-Jewish modernizers like General Mercier were thought to be in league with the Jews. The anti-modernizing impulse was inextricably linked with antisemitism.[32]

Marcel Thomas seems to me correct when he argues that the military brass did not consider Dreyfus guilty *only* because he was Jewish. "But the fact that he was Jewish led them to accept more easily than they would have for someone else the idea of his guilt."[33] In other words, because Dreyfus was a Jew, the officers investigating the case were not *surprised* that he would have committed treason once they saw the superficial similarity between his handwriting and that of the bordereau. Indeed, as soon as Sandherr was informed that Dreyfus was the suspect, he declared, "I should have known."[34] An avowed antisemite, Sandherr anticipated what the nationalist writer Maurice Barrès would proclaim several years later, at the height of the affair: "That Dreyfus is capable of treason, I conclude from his race."[35]

But as Thomas points out, the fact that Sandherr did *not* immediately suspect Dreyfus when they discovered the bordereau suggests that he did not automatically assume that the spy would be the one Jew on the General Staff.

In the week that followed, the investigators searched for evidence that might link Dreyfus to the crime. He had gone to Alsace on several occasions; he had always asked a lot of questions about munitions; and so on. This evidence was hardly conclusive and the investigators knew it. Their biggest problem was that there was no obvious motive for Dreyfus to commit treason. Because of his wealth, he had no need to sell secrets to Germany for money. To assume Dreyfus was guilty, they therefore had to impute to him more sinister motives: a desire to harm France.

It seems clear that the counterespionage team made this assumption because Dreyfus was Jewish. Du Paty de Clam, who was called in to help investigate on October 6 because of his supposed expertise in handwriting, even came close to admitting as much in his memoirs, while attempting to claim he was not an antisemite. "At that time, I was imbued with humanitarian prejudices, I had very good relations with intelligent Jews, artists, men of knowledge," he writes. In the next breath, however, he states that Dreyfus had no place on the General Staff: "There are situations where it is not a good idea to put people who are not unquestionably real Frenchmen [*des Français de France*]." Du Paty de Clam specifies that he did not consider Dreyfus a real Frenchman because of his Alsatian background and the German nationality of some of his relatives. But there were many non-Jewish Alsatians in the army, including Sandherr, and nobody questioned their loyalty to France.[36]

After Du Paty de Clam dictated the letter to Dreyfus on the morning of October 15 to see how he wrote certain words contained in the bordereau, he arrested him on the spot, barely consulting the handwriting sample. He had decided in advance that he had his man. Commandant Henry then emerged from behind the curtain where he had been hiding during the bizarre dictation scene. It was Henry who drove Dreyfus to the military prison, located on the site of a former convent on the rue du Cherche-Midi. According to Henry's testimony, Dreyfus protested wildly on the short journey: "My commandant, this is terrifying! I am accused of something horrible!" He said he would prefer a shot in the head to the torture of being falsely accused. "I am not guilty! . . . I understand that the Ministry would not have acted if it didn't have proof; it must be convincing for them and devastating for me, *but it is false* . . . I don't understand any of it! I demand justice!"[37]

The commander of the prison, Forzinetti, placed Dreyfus in an isolated cell, where he was prevented from seeing or communicating with the outside or even speaking to his guards. Forzinetti had been instructed by Colonel d'Aboville that such measures were necessary because of likely efforts by "High Jewry" (*haute juiverie*) to try to free him.[38] "I paced around my cell, banging my head against the walls," Dreyfus wrote in his memoir, describing his despair as he thought about the family he had left just a few hours before.[39]

He might have killed himself had Forzinetti not intervened. An experienced officer and one of the few to keep an open mind about Dreyfus's guilt, Forzinetti had seen a lot of accused criminals in his career, and Dreyfus did not strike him as acting like a guilty man. "I went to see Captain Dreyfus," he would later write. "He was in a state of terrible excitation; I had before me a true madman, with bloodshot eyes, who had knocked over all the furniture in his cell. I managed to calm him, but not without difficulty. I had the intuition that this officer was innocent." Forzinetti later testified to his belief in Dreyfus's innocence at trial.[40]

At the time, Forzinetti focused on preventing some of Du Paty de Clam's attempts to elicit a confession from the pris-

oner, which included waking Dreyfus up at odd hours and shin-
ing bright lights into his eyes. Unable to establish a motive for
the crime, Du Paty de Clam confronted Dreyfus with the rumors of his former romantic liaisons, hoping to find proof that
he led a secret life. He also questioned him about his travel to
Alsace and his contact with the German embassy. Dreyfus acknowledged once having sought a travel visa—he made his other
visits to Alsace clandestinely, as did many who had families across
the border. In his lengthy interrogations, Du Paty de Clam deliberately changed dates and facts to trip Dreyfus up. Dreyfus
managed to remain calm during these interviews, only giving
way to rage and despair when he returned alone to his cell.[41]

Meanwhile, Du Paty de Clam paid a visit to Lucie Dreyfus
to search the apartment. He told her only that her husband had
been arrested, refusing to reveal the reason or the place of detention, and forbidding her to inform anybody about the arrest,
even other family members. He returned several times over the
course of the next several days, confronting the distraught Lucie
with the rumors of her husband's infidelities and other bad hab-
its, including gambling. Stupefied by these sudden events, Lucie
nevertheless proclaimed her absolute faith in her husband's innocence. This faith never did waver. Though only twenty-five
years old at the time of her husband's arrest and having led a
sheltered existence, she maintained remarkable self-possession
in all her dealings with the military authorities. Eventually she
received permission to inform the rest of the family, and immediately summoned her brother-in-law Mathieu from Mulhouse.
Like Lucie, he never believed for a second that Alfred could
have committed treason and began arranging for his brother's
defense.

Over the course of the next six weeks, the military investigators tried to build a case against the man they had arrested
so precipitously. At first, they refused to tell Dreyfus what evidence they had of his crime, but eventually they showed him the

bordereau. To Dreyfus, the handwriting seemed quite different from his own. Having seen the bordereau, he could prove that he could not have been its author. He demonstrated that he had not "gone on maneuvers" in 1894, as the author of the letter stated he was about to do. He showed that he never had access to the information the spy offered to sell. Forzinetti reported that Dreyfus managed to remain in possession of his faculties during the entire ordeal of the investigation, hoping that he could eventually persuade his fellow officers of the truth.

Meanwhile, the case against Dreyfus began to fall apart. The Prefecture of Police withdrew its initial report concerning Dreyfus's gambling—they had mistaken him for someone else. But instead of admitting this mistake, Mercier suppressed the truth and proceeded with the investigation. It seems likely that pressure exerted by antisemitic newspapers forced him to do so. At first, no news about the case had leaked to the press. Then, on October 29, *La Libre parole* published a blind item alluding to an arrest for espionage and insinuating that a cover-up was taking place. Historians suspect that Commandant Henry leaked the information about the case to Drumont as he began to worry that Mercier would let Dreyfus go free. On October 31, the newspaper *Le Soir* revealed the identity of the accused: "the officer in question was named Dreyfus," it proclaimed. On November 1, the front page of *La Libre parole* announced: "High Treason. Arrest of the Jewish Officer A. Dreyfus." Given Drumont's relentless hounding of Mercier, his baseless claims that he had links to Jewish financiers, the minister of war felt he had no other option but to pursue the case despite the lack of evidence.[42]

Finally, on December 5, 1894, the military authorities officially charged Dreyfus with treason and allowed him to read the report they had assembled. They also allowed him to communicate with his family and with the lawyer, Edgar Demange, whom Mathieu Dreyfus had just engaged on his behalf. A conservative and a Catholic, Demange could not be suspected of being corrupted by Jewish influence. He agreed to represent Dreyfus only on the condition that he believe in his innocence. After finally being allowed to review the evidence—or lack thereof—Demange became convinced that the prosecution of Dreyfus was motivated by antisemitism. He took the case.[43]

The antisemitic press wasted no time in whipping up popular sentiment against the accused. "As a Jew and German, he detests the French," wrote *La Libre parole* two weeks after first naming Dreyfus. "A German by taste and upbringing, a Jew by race, he did the job of a Jew and a German—and nothing else."[44] The newspaper *La Croix*, published by the Assumptionists (a right-wing Catholic congregation), was even more vicious: "Jewry . . . has rotted out everything . . . it is a horrid cancer . . . the Jews are vampires . . . leading France into slavery." Both papers demanded that Jews be banished from France and published lists of Jewish military officers who should also fall under suspicion.[45]

As he awaited the court-martial in his prison cell, Dreyfus wrote letters to Lucie describing his disbelief at the charges and affirming unwavering patriotism: "Me, accused of the most monstrous crime a soldier could commit!"[46] He also used his time to prepare a detailed response to every element in the government's case, countering the baseless lies and innuendo with logic and facts. He assured his family that he would soon be set free. "I am approaching the end of my suffering, the end of my martyrdom. Tomorrow I will appear before my judges, my head high, my soul at ease," he wrote to Lucie the night before the trial.[47]

Dreyfus still did not understand the determination of his adversaries to see him convicted. The case had turned into a matter of state in which the honor and prestige of the military were on the line. Instead of backing down once it became clear that there was not enough evidence to obtain a conviction, the officers involved in the investigation grew determined to find more evidence. Schemes to cover up a mistake or a crime always seem inexplicable in retrospect, after they are exposed, but their perpetrators make a calculated gamble: they risk the possibility of future ignominy to avoid the certainty of shame in the present.

Henry combed through every piece of correspondence that had reached the Statistical Section and eventually found something he thought they could use. It was a letter by the German military attaché Schwarzkoppen to his Italian counterpart—and lover—Alessandro Panizzardi, whom he referred to affectionately in the feminine as *Alexandrine*, as well as his "dear little girl" and "bugger." The two exchanged many letters in this flirtatious style, which was well known to Henry and his colleagues in French counterintelligence. One of these letters enclosed some plans of French military fortifications that Schwarzkoppen said he had obtained from "that scoundrel D [*ce canaille de D*]." In fact, Henry knew this referred to a low-level French spy named Dubois, but he nevertheless placed it in a "secret dossier" that the military submitted to the judges during Dreyfus's court-martial as further proof of Dreyfus's guilt.[48]

The trial, which took place in a room in the Cherche-Midi prison, began on December 19, 1894. It lasted only three days. The military determined that the trial would proceed *in camera*, without the public present. Dreyfus could not lean on his family for support as he heard the military's lawyers detail all the sordid insinuations about his past that he had shown to be false. The judges were told that he bragged about his wealth, cavorted with women after his marriage, and said that Alsace was better off under German control.[49] Six of his fellow officers spoke in his defense, many of the others having assumed that their superiors could not be wrong about so grave a matter. Demange also called a series of character witnesses—including the Chief Rabbi of Paris, J.-H. Dreyfuss, no relation to the accused, and the philosopher Lucien Lévy-Bruhl, who was in fact a relation by marriage—but because they were Jews, the judges discounted their testimony.

Still, Dreyfus and his lawyer felt confident that they would win the case given the paucity of hard evidence against him. What they did not know was that the judges had seen the "secret dossier" containing the "scoundrel D" letter and other supposedly incriminating items. Not permitting the defense to examine evidence was a violation of the French legal code, even in military courts-martial, but the military managed to persuade the court that state security prevented the items in the "secret dossier" from being shown to anyone but the judges. The court returned a guilty verdict on December 22, 1894.[50]

Dreyfus experienced such shock when he learned of the verdict that his lawyer and family feared he would try to take his life in prison. Forzinetti had him watched day and night to make sure that he did not, but it was really Dreyfus's love for his wife and his family that gave him the courage to carry on. "It is for you alone that today I resist," he wrote to Lucie; "it is for you alone, my darling, that I withstand this long martyrdom."[51] On December 23, Chief Rabbi Zadoc Kahn requested permission to visit Dreyfus "to bring him the aid of religion," but his request was denied by the authorities, perhaps out of fear that the rabbi, as an agent of "High Jewry," would try to facilitate his escape.[52]

Lucie felt the blow as deeply as her husband. "What misfortune, torture, ignominy," she wrote him, vowing to devote herself to finding the real culprit. French law had outlawed the death penalty for political crimes such as treason in 1848, so Dreyfus faced perpetual deportation to a distant location. Finally allowed to see her husband on January 2, 1895, Lucie expressed a desire to follow him into exile with the children so at least they could remain together.[53]

First, though, he had to endure the ritual degradation ceremony, which Dreyfus referred to as "the horrible torture" and "the supreme humiliation" in letters to Lucie before the dreaded event. "I will resist, I promised you that," he wrote, perhaps as much to convince himself as to comfort his wife. "I will draw the force I still need in your love, in the affection of all of you . . . in the ultimate hope that the truth will one day come to light."[54]

The degradation took place on the morning of January 5— a Saturday, the Jewish sabbath. Dreyfus was brought to the École militaire an hour before the ceremony and made to wait in a small antechamber, watched by guards, as his fellow soldiers assembled in the courtyard and a massive crowd formed outside the gates. As he steeled all the force of his being for what was about to happen next, he tried to make sense of the ordeal he had undergone in the previous months. He still could not understand that his superior officers, the leaders of the army he so revered, could have allowed such a miscarriage of justice to take place.

As bells chimed nine o'clock, he was led into the vast courtyard. His comrades were assembled by regiment, according to plans that had been carefully mapped out, with artillery soldiers on one side and the calvary on the other. He felt the glare of their hatred as they confronted a man they believed was a traitor.[55]

The press corps, with reporters from around the world, scrutinized his face for any sign of guilt or remorse. He resolved to show them nothing but dignity. "I stiffened myself to concentrate all my strength," he later wrote. "To keep upright I recalled the memory of my wife, my children."[56] He managed to hold his head erect, his back straight. As soon as General Paul Darras read the verdict and declared him unfit to bear arms for France, Dreyfus turned to the assembled soldiers and cried out: "Soldiers, an innocent man is being degraded; soldiers, an innocent man is being dishonored. Long live France! Long live the Army!" But his cries were drowned out by shouts of "Down with the traitor!" and "Death to Judas!" If Dreyfus also heard shouts of "Down with the Jews!" and "Dirty Jew!" that certain newspapers reported, he didn't say.[57]

Le Petit Journal

Le Petit Journal
CHAQUE JOUR 5 CENTIMES

Le Supplément illustré
CHAQUE SEMAINE 5 CENTIMES

SUPPLÉMENT ILLUSTRÉ
Huit pages : CINQ centimes

ABONNEMENTS
TROISIÈME COLONNE 15 AS
PARIS .... 1 fr. 2 fr. 3 fr 50
DÉPARTEMENTS 1 fr. 2 fr. 4 fr
ÉTRANGER ...... 1 50 2 50 5 fr

Sixième année   DIMANCHE 13 JANVIER 1895   Numéro 217

LE TRAITRE
Dégradation d'Alfred Dreyfus

Cover of *Le Petit Journal, supplément illustré,* January 13, 1895
(Lorraine Beitler Collection of the Dreyfus Affair, Kislak Center for Special
Collections, Rare Books and Manuscripts, University of Pennsylvania)

A guard then approached and ripped the insignia from his uniform—the red stripes from his trousers and his epaulets, which had been loosened the night before. The guard took Dreyfus's sword and broke it over his knee. Dreyfus described feeling shock waves convulse his entire being as he saw "all these scraps of honor fall at my feet." Outwardly, though, he maintained his rigid bearing and continued to cry out "I am innocent! I am innocent!" to the hostile crowd.

How does an innocent man hold his head? How does he walk? How does he sound? Dreyfus must have asked himself these questions as the spectacle dragged on. "I had to make a tour of the courtyard," he wrote. "I heard the screams of the deluded crowd. I felt the emotion that made them vibrate because they were being confronted with a man condemned for treason, and I tried to make that crowd feel another emotion, that of my innocence."[58]

Whatever doubts about his guilt he may have instilled in the spectators assembled that day, they were quickly dispelled when one of the guards, Captain Charles Gustave Lebrun-Renault, reported to the press that Dreyfus had confessed to the crime as he waited for the ceremony to begin. "If I handed over documents, these documents had no value and it was only to get more important ones from the Germans," the guard reported hearing Dreyfus say.[59] Lebrun-Renault later recanted this testimony, but the legend of the confession took hold, assuaging the consciences of the few who remained unconvinced by the verdict.[60]

As the crowds dispersed from the École militaire that day, France and the world considered the Dreyfus case officially closed.

3

The Prisoner

DREYFUS COULD STILL HEAR the crowd calling for his death as he was escorted from the degradation ceremony to the police prefecture, where the authorities kept him isolated from the other prisoners for his own safety. The mug shots taken that day, according to the procedure established by the criminologist Alphonse Bertillon, show him still in his tattered army uniform. His eyes have a melancholy but dignified expression, and the downward curve of his moustache exaggerates the slight frown of his tightly closed lips (as seen in the frontispiece).

Later that afternoon, in his cell at the Prison de la Santé, he began drafting letters, the occupation that would help maintain his sanity during the difficult years to come. The style of these letters, which he knew would be read by the authorities, resembled the image he projected: a tightly composed surface masking the pain that lay beneath. To his lawyer Demange, he wrote, "As an innocent man, I endured the most awful martyrdom that one can inflict on a soldier," and vowed that although he would rather die, he would continue to live in order to bring the truth to light. He made a similar promise in a letter to his siblings: "I will live, as long as my forces allow, until they restore my honor to me." And to his wife, Lucie, whom he would write two or sometimes three times a day, he confided, "One day when we are happy again I will tell you what I suffered today." He asked her to do whatever she could to find the actual traitor: "This is my only hope amid the horrific sadness that engulfs me."[1]

Once they denied his appeal, the authorities had to decide where to imprison him. Dreyfus assumed he would be deported to the prison colony on Ducos Island, near New Caledonia, off the eastern coast of Australia. This is where the French sent most political prisoners, including those who had taken part in the Paris Commune in 1871. Deportees to New Caledonia were usually permitted to bring their families, and Dreyfus expressed relief in the knowledge that he would have Lucie to lean on during his exile. Having read his letters, however, General Mercier determined not to allow Dreyfus this comfort.

As they debated his destiny, the military decided to move him temporarily to an isolated fortress on the Île de Ré, an island off the west coast of France. Late in the night of January 17, 1895, the guards roused Dreyfus and brought him—half-dressed, his legs in chains, his hands cuffed—to the train station for the trip to La Rochelle, where he would await the boat to the fortress. Hoping to avoid crowds, they did not allow him to get off the train in La Rochelle, but the sight of the heavily guarded railroad car aroused suspicion at the station. Soon a crowd had assembled, and Dreyfus could hear it grow more agitated over the course of the day. When he finally exited the train that night, the police escort did not prevent the crowd from attacking him with canes and clubs while yelling "Death to the traitor! Death to the Jew!" Dreyfus reported feeling that the crowd, believing him a traitor, was justified in its wrath.[2]

Lucie Dreyfus finally obtained permission to visit her husband on the Île de Ré during the second week of February 1895. The prison authorities had forbidden her to reveal that the *Journal officiel* had already announced the ultimate place of his detention: Devil's Island, the smallest of the three so-called "Îles du Salut"—Salvation Islands—off the coast of French Guiana, in South America. First established in 1852, the penal colonies in French Guiana had proven so deadly—more than half of the prisoners sent there during the Second Empire died of yellow fever, malaria, and other tropical diseases—that the French had mostly stopped using them. But Mercier proposed a "law of exception" to allow the use of Devil's Island for Dreyfus, with the understanding that the remote location would make escape impossible, and the Chamber of Deputies voted its approval without debate. Prevented from executing the traitor by the abolition of the death penalty for political crimes, the military saw Devil's Island as the next best thing: Victor Hugo had called French Guiana "the dry guillotine."[3] Though the law permitted Lucie to join her husband in exile, her requests made to the minister of the colonies to do so received no reply. She returned to the Île de Ré a few weeks later, before her husband's departure, to bring him mosquito netting and other necessities for the journey.[4]

The voyage across the Atlantic took fifteen days, during which Dreyfus was kept in a kind of cage on the deck of the ship, exposed first to extreme cold, then to extreme heat. Although he was not told his destination, he managed to figure it out from the direction the ship was sailing and from some conversations overheard on deck. When he arrived in the main port on Royal Island, the largest of the Îles du Salut, on March 12, 1895, the temperature was 104 degrees. He needed help walking when he finally set foot on shore and was taken to the prison on Royal Island, where he was kept in an unventilated guard's room for more than a month while they readied Devil's Island for his arrival. Under orders to prevent his escape at all costs, and determined to maximize his suffering, the commander of the prison prevented Dreyfus from going outside. Other convicts brought him inedible food and carried away his waste. Soon he began to suffer from intestinal parasites, and the commander allowed him to consult a doctor, who prescribed quinine and a healthier diet. Dreyfus recovered enough to be transferred to Devil's Island on April 14, 1895.[5]

Surrounded by shark-infested waters, Devil's Island was the least hospitable of the three Salvation Islands and the most remote. Whereas the other two islands housed repeat offenders, attempted escapees, and the insane, only a small colony of lepers lived in the barren huts on Devil's Island, where they foraged for wild tomatoes and tended goats. The lepers had been hastily evacuated to make way for Dreyfus, who would now be the sole prisoner on the island. Confined to a small stone hut, about forty square feet, with two tiny windows blocked by iron bars, Dreyfus was watched day and night by a rotating team of guards, who had their own cabin a short distance away. The light from the guard's lantern glowed day and night, and the clanking of their keys, as they changed shifts every two hours during the night, made sleep impossible.[6]

His furniture consisted of an iron cot, a wood table, two cane-bottom chairs, a wash basin, and a bucket. He drew rancid water from a cistern that he used for drinking, cooking, and washing, and he soon developed dysentery. He might have been able to drink the milk of the wild goats on the island, but the commandant ordered the animals removed for fear that the prisoner would attempt to use one as a raft during an escape attempt. Supplied with unroasted coffee berries and raw meat, Dreyfus was forced to gather wood and build a fire if he wanted to consume them—although he was at first denied matches. With no utensils or cooking vessels, he resorted to using rusted cans of condensed milk abandoned by the lepers. After spending the better part of his days trying to cook in the burning heat, he resolved to live on bread and fetid water alone.[7]

In July 1895, he began receiving parcels with tins of preserved food from France, bought with 500 francs that Lucie placed into an account each month. He was eventually supplied with basic kitchen implements along with an iron mug; it was thought he might use glass as a weapon against the guards or himself. Although he makes no mention of observing kosher dietary laws, he repeatedly states in his journal that he tossed his ration of conserved lard (bacon) into the sea, even in the early days when he was literally starving.[8]

French penal colonies in the nineteenth century were among the most brutal places on earth. Intended to discipline rather than rehabilitate, they tormented prisoners not just with infernal temperatures and unsanitary conditions, but also with backbreaking labor like clearing the jungle and building roads. Though maintained by the supposedly liberal, democratic Third Republic, these penal colonies were instruments of state-run terror. In many ways, they forecast the concentration camp universe of the Nazis several decades later. As Stephen Toth has shown, the ordinary prisoners condemned to live in these colonies—often for decades, with no hope of parole or escape—developed various strategies for survival, and an entire penal colony culture evolved with its own customs and social hierarchies. But Dreyfus was not an ordinary prisoner.[9]

The ministry of war shared responsibility for Dreyfus's imprisonment with the ministry of the colonies, which had vast experience with dehumanizing indigenous populations in Africa. From the start, they determined that Dreyfus would be subject to a unique regime of total isolation, intended ostensibly to eliminate possibilities for escape but really to inflict maximum psychic stress. Spared the forced labor imposed on ordinary criminals, he was also denied the sanity-restoring benefits of human society. Since he was forbidden to communicate with his guards, who watched him at all times, Dreyfus essentially did not speak for his five years of detention and yet was never actually alone. By the time he returned to France for his retrial in 1899, he had nearly lost the use of his voice.

How did Dreyfus survive the ordeal? What coping mechanisms allowed him to persevere? First and foremost, he wrote. On sheets of paper that were numbered by the guards to make sure he did not attempt to use them to send secret messages, he began a journal of his "sad and sorrowful life." This journal, which would later be translated into dozens of languages and become a bestseller under the title *Cinq années de ma vie* (Five Years of My Life), records the thoughts and feelings of a man whose education in France's best schools had not prepared him for the arbitrary and cruel world into which he had been thrust.

"Until now," the journal begins on the night he arrived on Devil's Island, "I had adhered to the religion of reason, I believed in the logic of things and events and I believed in human justice! Everything that was bizarre or extravagant had difficulty entering my brain. Alas! What a complete collapse of all my beliefs." He struggled to understand the suspicion that surrounded him at all times in captivity, worse even than the material privations because it offended his sense of honor. "Ah! How I would like to live until the day of my rehabilitation in order to shout my sufferings," he wrote. "Will I make it until then? I often have doubts, so broken is my heart, so precarious is my health."[10]

Dreyfus's notebooks also contain hundreds of arabesque doodles, which were perhaps related to the problems of geometry and calculus that he tried to reconstruct from memory to ward off boredom and maintain his sanity. Michael Burns refers to these drawings as the "methodical hieroglyphics of a Polytechnicien walking the razor's edge of a nervous breakdown" and suggests that their abstraction reflected his desire for a more perfect world "above human passions," as Dreyfus put it in a letter to his wife.[11]

In addition to writing his journal, Dreyfus composed letters—to the military authorities, the president of the republic, his siblings, and most of all to Lucie. To the government, he proclaimed his innocence and decried the terrible infractions of law and human decency inflicted on him by the authorities. Like at the École militaire, when he registered complaints about antisemitism to his superiors, he maintained a firm belief that those in positions of power would eventually rectify the injustice he had suffered. To his family and Lucie, he poured out his soul, and Lucie scrutinized every missive for indications of his state of mind, which she constantly tried to cheer. "My dearest Fred," she would begin her letters back to him, which tried constantly to buoy his spirits. Fearing the military censors, she avoided talking about his case except in the most general terms, sticking instead to safe topics—past times they had enjoyed together, the children's education. "I share your suffering, your tortures, my poor dear one," she wrote. "I would give my life to relieve them." Each letter overflows with love.[12]

It is not an exaggeration to say that these letters kept him alive through the five-year ordeal. "When I write to my wife," he confided in his journal, "it is one of my rare moments of calm." In a letter to Lucie, he explained, "It seems to me, when I write to you, that the distances collapse, that I see your beloved face in front of me and that there is some part of you with me." At the same time, he knew that the letters were being read by the military authorities, and he encouraged Lucie to put on a courageous front: "to be brave and energetic because our honor must appear to everyone, without exception, what it has always been—pure and without a stain."[13] Both Alfred and Lucie felt an overwhelming need to exhibit decorum in the public face they presented. This was typical of their class and milieu—the Jewish bourgeoisie, who were striving to integrate into French culture and extremely conscious of playing a role. But it was especially true for the Dreyfuses because they knew that every word they wrote would be scrutinized by the authorities.

In addition to writing and drawing, Dreyfus read a great deal once he began receiving reading material in January 1896. It seems odd that his jailers permitted Lucie to send him books, given the otherwise extreme deprivation of his existence, but perhaps they didn't realize the kind of sustenance someone of Dreyfus's contemplative cast of mind could derive from the written word. Books became a kind of lifeline, a link to a world beyond his desert island. Dreyfus read for instruction, to improve himself, and also to gain insight into the human condition. Alongside the *Revue des deux mondes* and the *Revue de Paris*, scientific journals, and textbooks of literary and art history, he read Montaigne, whose philosophical *Essays* acknowledged suffering as the basis of the human condition but found joy in friendship and freedom in thought. He also loved Shakespeare and devoted at least two to three hours per day to improving his English so he could read it in the original. Iago's lines in *Othello* had particular resonance for him, and he translated them in a letter to Lucie:

> Who steals my purse steals trash; 'tis
> something, nothing;
> 'Twas mine, 'tis his, and has been slave
> to thousands:
> But he that filches from me my good name
> Robs me of that which not enriches him
> And makes me poor indeed. (Act 3, Scene 3)

Soon he settled into a kind of routine. He would rise at daybreak, around 5:30 in the morning, and head outside before the heat of the sun became oppressive. Allowed to circulate in a small part of the island (about two thousand square feet), he would build a fire in order to make coffee or tea and cook some dried beans. Then he would wash himself and make his bed. At

8 A.M., he received his daily ration of food. If it contained meat, he would cook it immediately (except for the bacon), while the fire remained lit. He spent the hottest hours of the day inside reading and writing. Once the sun had begun to set, he would cut wood and eat what he had cooked that morning. The worst part of the day came when they locked him in his cell after dinner. Without sufficient light to read, he could not distract himself from his mental anguish. As he put it in his journal, "I am reduced to going to bed, and it is then that my brain begins to work, that all my thoughts turn toward the terrible drama of which I am the victim, and all my thoughts go toward my wife, my children, and those who hold me dear. How they too must suffer!"[14]

His hut swarmed with all kinds of insects, and his body was covered with their bites. He experienced recurrent bouts of fever. "But all that is nothing!" he wrote in his journal. "What is physical suffering next to my horrible moral tortures?" He could not stand to think that the world considered him guilty while the real traitor went free. He vowed to see justice done and his honor restored. "Will I live until then? I sometimes doubt it when I feel my whole being dissolve in terrible despair." But then the thought of his wife and children would come back to him, and he would find the strength to carry on.[15]

The Dreyfus scholar Vincent Duclert considers his will to live in the face of unbearable suffering to be nothing short of heroic. In contrast to a long-standing tendency among historians to dismiss Dreyfus as a marginal figure in his own affair because he played no role in the political struggle waged on his behalf, Duclert sees Dreyfus as the model of resistance to the kind of state-sanctioned violence against individuals—and particularly against Jewish individuals—that later marked the totalitarian regimes of the twentieth century. Indeed, it was only because of Dreyfus's stubborn determination to survive his torture that the political struggle to free him could take place. I see Dreyfus's heroism in much the same way. If abstract concepts like truth and justice emerged victorious at the end of the affair, if France was able to affirm its commitment to human rights in general, it was only because of the will of this particular man to resist—day by day, over a period of five years—extreme physical hardship and material privation. If Dreyfus had given up, the forces of reaction would have triumphed, with devastating consequences for twentieth-century French politics.[16]

Dreyfus's journal and letters make clear that he understood the significance of his resistance. In his very first journal entry, written on April 14, 1895, the day of his transfer to Devil's Island, he describes his desire to die after his unjust condemnation: "this was certainly enough to drive a man who placed honor above all to despair." But he came to realize, thanks in large part to Lucie, that "as an innocent man, I did not have the right to abandon or voluntarily desert my post." What Dreyfus would refer to as his *devoir*, his duty, consisted in fighting against a corrupt system that could condemn an innocent man on flimsy evidence. Survival was never just a personal matter for him. When he said that he did not have the right to give up, he meant not just for himself or his family, but for France, and by extension for the world—since the world looked to France as a model of democratic values. "It is necessary that I struggle," he wrote, "that I always resist."[17]

Through it all, Dreyfus maintained faith that truth would prevail, that the system would correct itself and halt the slide toward tyranny. This is clear in a letter he wrote to the president of the republic, Félix Faure, in October 1895, from his insect-infested hut on Devil's Island, forgotten by the world and deprived of the most basic forms of sustenance, but not of his dignity or his belief in justice.

> For the past year, I have struggled, alone with my conscience, against the most horrible fate that can befall a man . . .

I solicit neither pardon, nor favor, nor moral sympathy. I ask, I beg, that the full and entire light of day be shone on those machinations of which I and my family are the unhappy and horrible victims.

If I have lived, Monsieur le Président, if I manage still to live, it is because the sacred duty that I have sworn to my loved ones to uphold fills my soul and governs it; otherwise, I would have already succumbed beneath a load too heavy for human shoulders to bear.

In the name of my honor torn away by a horrifying error, in the name of my wife, in the name of my children—oh! Monsieur le Président, that last thought alone makes the heart of a father, of a Frenchman, of an honest man roar with sadness—I demand of you justice, and that justice I demand of you, with all my soul, with all the strength of my heart, with hands joined in a supreme prayer, is to cast light on this tragic story, and to put an end to the horrifying martyrdom of a soldier and of a family for whom honor is everything.[18]

Dreyfus may have had no knowledge of the affair that was taking place without him, but he most certainly understood what his case meant for France and for humanity. Though he received a response marked simply "Rejected without comment," his plea to the president was not the futile effort of a deluded man, but rather the indication of his continued belief in a more just and honorable world, one that only his daily struggle could bring about.[19]

If eventually the movement to free Dreyfus would mobilize a large segment of the French population, at first it was only a tiny band of devoted supporters who believed in his innocence. First among these was Lucie. In the initial days following his arrest, she was quite literally alone in her struggle and anguish: as he ransacked her home to find proof of her husband's treachery, Commandant du Paty de Clam threatened that if she breathed a word of the arrest to anyone, even close family members, her husband would be doomed. Over the next five years, as the movement to free her husband grew, she remained his most important supporter. It was she who fought with the military authorities to exercise her right to join her husband in exile, and then when that was forbidden to her—in violation of the law— she fought to maintain contact, to see that her letters and parcels arrived on Devil's Island despite the government's desire to deprive the convict of all physical and moral sustenance. Although she eventually received adulation around the world as a symbol of wifely devotion—profiles in the American press focused especially on this aspect of her character—in the early days after her husband's condemnation, Lucie and the rest of the Dreyfus family were shunned by all but their closest relatives and friends.[20]

As soon as she was given permission to inform other members of the family of her husband's situation, Lucie reached out to Mathieu, Alfred's suave older brother, who had settled in Mulhouse to help run the family business. He joined her in Paris and immediately set about attempting to understand what had led to his brother's inexplicable arrest. "I never doubted for a second his total and absolute innocence," Mathieu would write. "I knew his perfect loyalty, his character, his good and bad qualities, his taste for work, his passion for the military profession." The lawyer Demange warned Mathieu that he risked being arrested as his brother's accomplice. Mathieu realized that he was being followed by government agents and that all his correspondence was being opened. He therefore resolved to work behind the scenes, with as much discretion as possible, to secure his brother's release.[21]

He faced serious obstacles. Knowing that they had a weak case, General Mercier and other members of the army high command devoted all their energy to making sure that the evidence—or lack thereof—remained secret. They were especially concerned to conceal the fact that the case rested on a

superficial similarity between Dreyfus's handwriting and that
of the bordereau, along with various circumstantial allegations
concerning Dreyfus's character, most of which had been proved
false. The military trial had been conducted behind closed doors
to prevent this lack of evidence from becoming public, and
even Demange was unaware that a "secret dossier" had been
shown to the judges. To conceal these machinations, Mercier
let it be known that the evidence against Dreyfus was so explosive that war with Germany would certainly follow should it
come to light, and he proposed a law to punish the publication
of classified documents with a five-year prison sentence.[22]

The Dreyfus family suspected from the beginning that
antisemitism lay behind the accusation, but also realized that
openly accusing the army of antisemitism risked fanning the
flames of a hatred that was all too ready to see the Jews as un-
patriotic. Shortly after Dreyfus's trial, *La Croix* described the
Jews as "parasites living off the substance of others, worthy of
toleration at best when they are neither too numerous nor too
influential and deserving to be chased out when their presence
becomes a threat."[23] Almost immediately, rumors spread that
a "Jewish syndicate" was attempting to manipulate public opinion and the levers of power to secure Dreyfus's release. One
police report that made its way into the "secret dossier" shown
to Dreyfus's judges noted that "The Jewish clan has become in-
credibly active in the attempt to mitigate the crime committed
by one of its own." Another such report noted, "In newspaper
offices, it is whispered that the House of Rothschild has de-
ployed its agents" on behalf of the accused man.[24]

Several legislators proposed antisemitic laws in the months
following Dreyfus's conviction. In late 1894, a deputy named
Fernand-René du Breil de Pontbriand put forth a law barring all
those whose ancestors had not held French citizenship for three
generations from government positions and elected office—
a measure with clear antisemitic intent. In the spring of 1895,

another deputy proposed forcing Jews to move to "the center of France, where treason is less dangerous." Alfred-Joseph Naquet, a Jewish deputy already well known—and hated by conservative Catholics—for sponsoring the law that had legalized divorce in France, took to the podium to protest but was drowned out by right-wing deputies. Although these antisemitic measures got voted down, they reveal that Jewish equality was far more precarious in France than many in the Jewish community wanted to believe.[25]

It was in this atmosphere of escalating intolerance that the popular writer Émile Zola penned his first article relating to the Dreyfus case. Known for his scandalous novels exposing social problems like alcoholism and prostitution, Zola had an immense following in France, and his words carried great weight. Entitled "A Plea for the Jews" and published in *Le Figaro* on May 16, 1896, Zola's article did not mention Dreyfus specifically, but rather took aim at the rise of antisemitism in France. "For a few years now, I have been following the campaign that they are trying to wage against the Jews with a growing surprise and disgust."[26] Calling antisemitism "something stupid and blind," and a throwback to the barbarism of the Middle Ages, Zola intended to defend the Jews against accusations of greed and treachery. He nevertheless recycled various antisemitic stereotypes. He asserted that Jews did indeed possess superior skill at making money but denied that they should be punished for their talents. According to Zola, rather than condemning Jews for their prowess, Christians should learn to compete with them and beat them at their own game. Readers at the time seem not to have perceived the author's ambivalence—especially not Drumont, who accused Zola in the pages of *La Libre parole* of pandering to the Jews.[27]

Given this climate, it seems natural that French Jews would have reacted to the news of Dreyfus's arrest and conviction with trepidation. One of their own had been found guilty of the worst crime imaginable. He had betrayed France to its enemy. He had sold out the nation that had been so generous to the Jews, that had been the first in Europe to make Jews citizens. Dreyfus seemed to have proven Drumont right. Who could blame French Jews for wanting to dissociate themselves from a man and a case that was so very bad for their community, who seemed to put their own livelihoods—perhaps even their own lives—at risk?

And yet, the French Jewish community has received a great deal of blame for its purported lack of solidarity with Dreyfus, both during the affair and after. In his speech to the Second Zionist Congress in 1898, Max Nordau—like his friend Theodor Herzl, an Austro-Hungarian journalist based in Paris—lambasted the French Jewish community for its passivity in the affair. In contrast to the antisemitic myth of an all-powerful "syndicate" of wealthy French Jews fighting to free Dreyfus, Nordau argued that French Jews lacked a sense of Jewish solidarity: "But we have fallen far short of the expectations of even those who hate and despise us most, and hence this tragic Dreyfus case has become a shockingly precise measure of the degree which our weakness, faintheartedness, obtuseness and mutual alienation has attained." It was the weakness of the French Jews during the affair that underscored the need for a Jewish state, according to Nordau.[28]

Non-Jewish Dreyfusards, such as Charles Péguy, came to echo this Zionist critique. In his influential tome *Notre jeunesse* (Our Youth), published in 1910, Péguy faulted French Jewish leaders for turning their backs on Dreyfus for the sake of maintaining peace with antisemites. A fervent Catholic—one of the few who would become a Dreyfusard—Péguy disapproved of any commitment that smacked of self-interest or "politics" rather than the more noble "mystique" that motivated his own engagement in the affair.[29]

In the decades that followed, the charge that French Jews remained silent during the affair continued to gain currency, especially among those wishing to underscore the link between Dreyfus and the fate of European Jewry during the Nazi period. Writing in 1935, immediately following Dreyfus's death, the future Socialist prime minister Léon Blum recalled how in his middle-class Jewish milieu there was barely "the slightest predisposition to Dreyfusism" after Dreyfus's arrest: "A great misfortune had befallen Israel. We suffered it without saying a word, hoping for time and silence to wipe away its effects." According to Blum, French Jews were especially intent on not appearing to defend Dreyfus because he was Jewish: "They didn't want people to attribute their attitude to racial distinction or solidarity." And they didn't want to risk fanning the flames of antisemitism.[30]

Blum published his *Souvenirs sur l'Affaire* (Memories of the Affair) when Hitler was consolidating power in Germany, and he is clear about the parallels he drew between the 1890s and the 1930s. "Rich Jews, middle-class Jews, Jews who were state functionaries were afraid of the fight on behalf of Dreyfus exactly the way they are afraid today of the fight against fascism."[31] His historical analogy was later taken up by Jewish historians after World War II, especially by Hannah Arendt, for whom the alleged passivity of French Jews during the Dreyfus Affair foreshadowed the flawed response of Europe's Jews to the Nazi threat. In *The Origins of Totalitarianism*, published in 1951, Arendt famously called the Dreyfus Affair the "dress rehearsal for the performance of our time," and she was brutal in her condemnation of French Jews, who she claimed were too concerned about their social standing to lift a finger on behalf of the unjustly condemned man. "Was not the sole desire of the Jews to continue to be accepted in society and suffered in the armed forces?" Arendt asked. For this German Jewish refugee from the Nazis, it was only non-Jews like Picquart and Clemenceau, and a small number of Jewish "pariahs," who fought to save the French republic from its slide into tyranny during the affair.[32]

But were French Jews really so timid? Were they really so ready to believe Dreyfus guilty or, worse, to believe him innocent and still to refuse to fight on his behalf? It is true that the majority of French Jews—like the majority of all French people—at first believed that the army must have had sufficient evidence to accuse Dreyfus and find him guilty. To forestall any accusations of Jewish solidarity with the accused traitor, *La Vraie parole*, the Jewish newspaper founded to combat antisemitism, called for Dreyfus to be shown no mercy. Isidore Singer, its editor, even suggested that he should be subjected to "the pitiless penal code of Moses," a death by stoning, with the Chief Rabbi of France casting the first stone.[33] Certain historians have maintained, however, that French Jews continued to be as timid in the period that followed. Michael Marrus, for example, maintains that with very few exceptions, Jewish journalists were afraid to confront the rising tide of antisemitism and failed to refute the charges that the Jewish community was full of traitors.[34]

The truth is more complicated. On one hand, it is true that the Consistory, the body that regulated Jewish religious practice in France, remained silent on the topic of the affair. As part of the official government bureaucracy, it could not criticize the military. Likewise, the Alliance Israélite Universelle, which advocated for the rights of Jews abroad, saw a domestic matter like the affair as beyond its purview. On the other hand, various nongovernmental French Jewish organizations—and many individual Jews, including some involved with the Consistory and the Alliance—defended Dreyfus and Jewish interests during the affair.[35]

Notably, even in the early days after the revelation of Dreyfus's arrest, the French Jewish press did not keep silent. The first article in *Les Archives israélites* to mention Dreyfus's name, on November 8, 1894, noted the "salutary reaction" that followed the initial burst of antisemitism in the press and praised those journalists who kept a level head.[36] An article from the week before the trial in December expressed hope that Dreyfus would be found innocent and called for all the evidence against Dreyfus to be brought into the open: "This affair must be liquidated in the full light of day."[37] Five days after the verdict came down, a mournful editorial by Isidore Cahen, the editor of *Les Archives israélites*, decried the antisemitism that threatened the French Jewish community as a result of the case. Even while sounding the alarm, however, Cahen expressed confidence that the same judicial system that had found Dreyfus guilty would protect Jewish rights.[38] *L'Univers israélite*, for its part, raised doubts about Dreyfus's guilt after the verdict and denounced the antisemitism that followed from it: "What is odious and must revolt every honest conscience is the conduct of those unfortunates who exploit the condemnation of a Jew in order to accuse all the Jews."[39]

If some French Jews rushed to distance themselves from the supposed traitor, others maintained from the beginning that he must be innocent. The latter group included Joseph Reinach. A brilliant polymath and committed republican, from a very wealthy and scandal-ridden family, Reinach was a deputy representing the Basses-Alpes region of France and would himself become the target of a great deal of antisemitism during the affair. He became one of the first to join the Dreyfusard cause. In his history of the affair, Reinach describes how "from the first day, I had the intuition that the accused man was innocent," because Dreyfus could have had no motive for the crime. Reinach's sense of the absurdity of the accusation was only strengthened by the vitriol with which Dreyfus was denounced by the nationalist and Catholic press—a sure sign that antisemitism was at work.[40] Joseph Reinach was soon joined in his certainty of Dreyfus's innocence by his equally brilliant brothers, Salomon and Théodore, who went on to militate in favor of the innocent man. Other leading Jewish politicians, such as Alfred-Joseph Naquet and his fellow deputy Camille Dreyfus, would also speak out against antisemitism during the affair. It is thus simply not true, even early on, that no French Jews supported Dreyfus.[41]

The accusation that the official French Jewish community remained passive during the affair is also belied by the fact that the leader of that community—Chief Rabbi Zadoc Kahn—took such an active role in the case. Kahn had made public declarations against antisemitism in the early 1890s, in response to the attacks by Drumont, but when Dreyfus was arrested, he went to work behind the scenes. A friend of the Hadamard family, Kahn had performed the wedding ceremony of Alfred and Lucie, and he shared the family's conviction that Dreyfus could not have committed treason. Made aware of the arrest, he immediately reached out to government officials—including the prefect of police and the minister of the interior—on Dreyfus's behalf. The Chief Rabbi remained very close to Mathieu Dreyfus and continued to play an important role as the movement for justice gained steam.[42]

It was Zadoc Kahn who assembled a Committee of Defense Against Antisemitism that included leading members of the Jewish community—including Baron Edmond de Rothschild and Narcisse Leven, the president of the Alliance Israélite Universelle. This committee funded numerous Dreyfusard groups as well as articles and brochures opposing antisemitism. The existence of the committee remained secret until 1902 to avoid fueling anti-Dreyfusard paranoia about a "Jewish Syndicate" controlling the levers of power. Indeed, Philippe Oriol speculates that the committee may have planted erroneous articles in the Jewish press accusing powerful Jews of doing nothing to support Dreyfus in order to hide its activities. Oriol suggests that it was these false reports that lay at the origin of the myth of Jewish "passivity" during the affair.[43]

If the support of Jewish community leaders for Dreyfus had to remain mostly clandestine, other Jews played a very public role in the fight for justice. In fact, nearly all of the first Drey-fusards were Jews (although certain Protestant intellectuals, like the historian Gabriel Monod, would soon join the fight). The most significant of these early Jewish defenders of Dreyfus was undoubtedly the journalist Bernard Lazare. Born Lazare Ber-nard in 1865 in Nîmes to a family of acculturated textile manu-facturers, Lazare had made a name for himself as an avant-garde writer and anarchist firebrand in Parisian literary circles by the early 1890s. In 1894—the year Dreyfus was arrested and con-demned—he published a study titled *Antisemitism: Its History and Its Causes*, which blamed the hatred of Jews on Jews them-selves, especially unassimilated Jewish immigrants from Eastern Europe. At this early stage in his career, Lazare saw the gradual decline of the Jewish religion, along with Socialist revolution, as a solution to the problem of antisemitism. No less a critic than Drumont called it a "remarkable book."[44] However, Lazare would undergo a radical transformation over the course of the Drey-fus Affair: his recognition of the intractability of the problem of antisemitism led him to become one of the first French Jews to embrace Zionism.[45]

In the year following his brother's condemnation, when in-terest in the case began to wane, Mathieu Dreyfus decided to engage a journalist to call attention to the miscarriage of justice that had taken place. At the advice of family friends, he con-tacted Lazare. At first, the anarchist showed no interest in the case, telling his editor, "If he were some poor devil, I would be worried for him. But Dreyfus and his family are very rich, they say; they'll be able to take care of themselves very well without me, especially if he is innocent." Nevertheless, he wrote several articles attacking the antisemitism that surfaced during the trial, and he eventually agreed to meet with Mathieu. Shocked at the lack of evidence that had sent Dreyfus to Devil's Island, Lazare overcame his political qualms and agreed to work on behalf of his wealthy co-religionist.[46]

Although he didn't have access to most of the documents pertaining to the case, Lazare was able to reconstruct the main outlines of the army's effort to frame Dreyfus. By the spring of 1895, he had completed a forceful pamphlet exposing the injustice of the arrest and trial. However, Mathieu had now become convinced that they should avoid creating a scandal and instead work behind the scenes to win important politicians over to their cause. He insisted on delaying publication of Lazare's pamphlet. Frustrated by this circumspection, Lazare nevertheless deferred to the family's wishes, which may have placed a brake on the wheels of justice. When it was eventually published in November 1896, Lazare's pamphlet played a decisive role in turning the tide of the affair.

If Lazare altered the outcome of the affair, the affair also changed the course of Lazare's life. Over the following years, until his early death from cancer in 1903, Lazare would be quite literally consumed by the case, which radically altered his understanding of the so-called Jewish Question. Whereas he had previously advocated for assimilation as the solution to the problem of antisemitism, and believed only the poor, orthodox Jews were threatened by it, the victimization of a wealthy, integrated Jew like Dreyfus changed his views. "I will never forget what I suffered in my Jewish flesh [*ma chair de juif*] on the day of your degradation," Lazare wrote to Dreyfus after reading his autobiography, *Cinq années de ma vie.* "You represented for me my entire race, martyred and insulted." As a result of the antisemitism unleashed during the affair, Zionism came to seem the only possible solution to the "Jewish Question." And the affair also caused him to develop a deeper, more mystical notion of Jewish identity in response. "From one day to the next," he wrote, "I became a pariah."[47]

The anarchist who had previously seen the world through the prism of the Marxist class struggle now came to recognize a desire for justice within the Jewish tradition. And he saw Dreyfus as the incarnation of that desire. "You are perhaps more Jewish than you know," he told the rationalist Dreyfus; "through your unflinching hope, your faith in something better, your almost fatalistic resignation. It is this indestructible principle that comes to you from your people, and it is this that has sustained you. A Christian, you would have died praying for divine justice. A Jew, you wanted to live to bring it about." Although he employed far more metaphysical language than Dreyfus himself would have used, Lazare was one of the first to recognize the heroism of Dreyfus's struggle. He was also one of the first to recognize both the significance of Judaism to that struggle and the significance of the struggle for Judaism.[48]

For Péguy, analyzing Lazare's transformation, he was one of the few who understood the true "mystique" of the affair. For Arendt, who mistakenly called Lazare "almost the only Jew in this movement for the liberation of a Jew," he represented the model of the "conscious pariah," who unlike his "parvenu" co-religionists, was willing to sacrifice everything for the sake of justice and for the sake of his people.[49] By pointing out that Lazare was not the only French Jew in the Dreyfusard movement, my goal is not to detract from Lazare's heroism. He did in fact play a heroic role, but he was far from the only Jew to do so. As we will see, the fight to free Dreyfus eventually became a cause célèbre within the French Jewish community, especially once Lazare published his pamphlet.[50] At that point, many French Jews became actively and publicly involved in the fight for justice, whether by signing petitions, attending trials, joining the Human Rights League, or, in the case of the Group of Jewish Socialist Workers of Paris, staging demonstrations on behalf of Dreyfus.[51]

Of course, Dreyfus had no inkling that anyone was fighting on his behalf as he confronted the fiendish conditions of Devil's Island. He was cut off not just from his family, but from any news about his case or about political developments back in France.

Later, when he learned of all those—both Jews and Christians—who had made sacrifices for his cause, he would be overwhelmed with gratitude. But on Devil's Island, each day, each hour, was a struggle simply to stay alive. And this was a battle that he had to fight alone.

4

The Affair

By the beginning of 1896, almost everyone had forgotten about Dreyfus, and his family despaired of ever finding proof of his innocence. Not knowing where else to turn, Mathieu Dreyfus even consulted a medium in the hope that her occult powers would lead him to overlooked evidence. Outside of the Dreyfus family, only a small band of supporters kept the struggle alive. Most of France had moved on.[1]

In March 1896, the Statistical Section—the military intelligence service—received another delivery from the "ordinary track," the trash collected from the German embassy by a cleaning woman who worked as a French spy. It was via this route that they had discovered the bordereau, the document revealing that a French officer had been selling secrets to Germany, which led to Dreyfus's arrest. The new delivery contained fragments of a telegram intended to be sent through the system of pneumatic tubes that crisscrossed Paris. This type of communiqué was referred to as a *petit bleu* because it was written on a special kind of thin blue paper. It contained the following cryptic message: "Sir, Above all I await a more detailed explanation than the one you gave me the other day of the question in abeyance. Consequently, I am requesting you to give it to me in writing so I may judge if I can continue my relations with the R. house or not. Signed: C."[2] This was the kind of coded language that the German military attaché, Schwarzkoppen (who often signed his letters "C"), used to communicate with French spies in his employ. The message, which was possibly a draft since it had not actually been sent, was addressed to a French officer named Ferdinand Walsin Esterhazy, who resided at 27, rue de la Bienfaisance in Paris.

When Commandant Georges Picquart, the new head of the Statistical Section, received the reconstituted document, he assumed the French army must have another traitor in its ranks. He immediately began investigating Esterhazy. If Dreyfus's background and personality made him a very unlikely candidate to commit treason—his wealth, for one thing, obviated the need to sell military secrets to the enemy—Esterhazy practically had the word "spy" written across his forehead. From a minor, illegitimate branch of a Hungarian noble family that had migrated to France in the seventeenth century, Esterhazy was a gambler and a womanizer. Unlike Dreyfus, he lacked a private income, which meant that he had amassed significant debts. As we saw, Esterhazy had agreed to serve as the second for André Crémieu-Foa, the Jewish officer who fought a duel against Drumont, and then attempted to extort money from the Rothschilds and other wealthy Jews as a recompense. As later emerged, he also duped some of his own relatives into giving him money that he claimed he was investing with the Rothschild bank but kept for himself. Esterhazy even looked the part of the villain, with beady black eyes, sunken cheeks, and a prodigious walrus moustache.[3]

In order to meet his escalating need for cash, Esterhazy had offered his services to Schwarzkoppen in June 1893, appearing at the German embassy brazenly, in broad daylight. Schwarzkoppen was suspicious at first of this outlandish character, who loudly proclaimed his hatred of France and his desire to serve its enemies, suspecting him at first of attempting to become a double agent. But after Esterhazy gave him some authentic documents relating to French artillery in the days that followed, Schwarzkoppen agreed to pay him a fixed sum every month in exchange for whatever information he could procure.

When Picquart set his eyes on the petit bleu, he had only recently taken over the intelligence service, after its former director, Colonel Sandherr, became ill from late-stage syphilis. Picquart was an Alsatian Catholic and a graduate of Saint-Cyr. Like many officers of his background, including Sandherr, he was an antisemite. Dreyfus had been his student at the École de guerre, and the ambitious Jewish officer had not made a favorable impression. Charged with assigning interns to divisions of the General Staff, Picquart apologized to the officer who would command Dreyfus for "giving him a Jew."[4] When the army accused Dreyfus of spying, Picquart had no difficulty believing him guilty. However, unlike his other antisemitic colleagues on the General Staff, Picquart did not allow his personal distaste for Jews to interfere with his duties. When his investigation turned up some of Esterhazy's recent letters and Picquart recognized the handwriting as identical to that of the bordereau—which meant that Esterhazy had committed the crime for which Dreyfus was being punished—he began working to rectify what he saw as a grave judicial error.

Picquart brought the evidence to his superiors, Generals de Boisdeffre and Gonse, expecting them to begin the process of reversing the judgment against the Jewish officer. Instead, the generals expressed little surprise at the proof of Dreyfus's innocence, and only seemed concerned that Picquart had been able to examine the bordereau, which they believed had been burned along with the rest of the file that had been secretly shown to Dreyfus's judges, in violation of the rules of criminal procedure. Boisdeffre and Gonse did not explicitly tell Picquart to stop his investigation of Esterhazy, but they instructed him to keep the Esterhazy and Dreyfus cases separate, signifying that they had no desire to see Dreyfus go free.

All of this happened, of course, without the knowledge of Mathieu and Lucie Dreyfus, who continued to receive heart-rending missives from the prisoner on Devil's Island. In a desperate move to reawaken interest in the case, Mathieu planted a false report in English newspapers that his brother had escaped. He planned to deny the rumor immediately but imagined that in the process he could at least attract attention to his brother's suffering. On September 3, 1896, the *Daily Chronicle* ran with the news of "the escape of Captain Dreyfus," and on September 4, the French government issued a denial after telegraphing to make sure that no escape had occurred. To a certain extent, Mathieu's plan worked: on September 8, *Le Figaro* published an article describing the appalling conditions on the island and the prisoner's fragile state of health.

But Mathieu's plan had unintended consequences as well. Concerned that efforts were afoot to facilitate Dreyfus's escape, the commandant of the Salvation Island prison received orders to heighten security. On September 6, the guards began chaining Dreyfus at night using the "double buckle": an iron contraption that locked the prisoner's ankles to the bed. Dreyfus could not move at all during the night, even when bugs crawled across his face and body or sores developed from remaining too long in the same position. Mystified by this new torture, Dreyfus was told that it was not a punishment, but a "security measure." Unable to sleep, racked with pain, he expressed in his journal his continued resolve to survive in order to "shed the brightest light possible on this terrifying drama." He also expressed pity for his torturers, imagining their guilt when his innocence was finally revealed: "What remorse lies in store for them once there is light?" he mused, "Because history knows no secrets." A few days later, "so exhausted, so broken in body and spirit" that he feared the loss of his sanity, he decided to stop writing in his journal.[5]

What Dreyfus could not have known was that at the moment of his greatest despair, the movement to free him was about to gain steam. On September 10, 1896, the newspaper *L'Éclair* published an article that was hostile to Dreyfus, urging the military to reveal "on what irrefutable grounds the Court-Martial based its decision" to find him guilty. Dreyfus's family immediately seized on this sentence as confirmation of what they had long suspected: that the judges had been shown a secret file, which would mean that his trial had been illegal. It is still not known who planted this story. Some suspected the Dreyfus family of planting it themselves to see how the army would react. More likely, it came from Commandant Henry, the officer in the Statistical Section who had assisted Du Paty de Clam in constructing the case against Dreyfus, who believed that he needed to tamp down any sympathy for the traitor by alluding to overwhelming evidence of his guilt. A few days later, *L'Éclair* published another article specifying that the judges at Dreyfus's court-martial had in fact been shown a letter written in code that the army had kept secret for national security reasons.

The document in question was the letter referring to a "scoundrel D [*canaille de D*]" who was growing too demanding, exchanged between the German military attaché Schwarzkoppen and his Italian counterpart and lover, Alessandro Panizzardi. The article in *L'Éclair* exaggerated the specificity of the letter— the newspaper quoted the letter as containing the phrase "that animal Dreyfus," when it had actually contained only the initial of the supposed spy. But now the supporters of Dreyfus knew for sure that his trial had been illegal because it had turned on documents that had not been shown to Dreyfus's lawyers. This was a violation even of military jurisprudence. Armed with this evidence, on September 18, Lucie Dreyfus petitioned the president of the Chamber of Deputies for a reversal of the verdict against her husband.

Jean-Denis Bredin argues that "the affair" began at this moment. He distinguishes between the judicial case involving Dreyfus, which commenced with his arrest in 1894, and the full-blown affair, which started once the effort to overturn the verdict against him became a popular movement. Although the judicial case involved only the army and the close band of supporters around Dreyfus, the affair eventually grew to encompass large sectors of the French population. France became divided between Dreyfusards and anti-Dreyfusards, as the two sides came to be known. And onlookers throughout the world kept abreast of the developments in the affair thanks to the burgeoning of daily newspapers, which covered the twists and turns on their front pages throughout the final years of the nineteenth century.[6]

What had begun as a case of petty espionage came to seem an event of global importance, because more than the fate of a single man was at stake: the Dreyfus Affair offered the first real test of the liberal institutions that had developed in the West over the course of the previous century. Could the rights of the individual compete against the interests of the military and state bureaucracy? Would the justice system prove independent of the pressure of the military and popular prejudice? Did equality before the law truly apply to every citizen, regardless of race and creed?

The fact that the man at the center of the affair was a Jew was not an incidental matter, since Jews offered liberal democracies a test of their inclusivity. The French Revolution had emancipated the Jews at the end of the eighteenth century to demonstrate the universality of the new system of government. In most other countries, the struggle for Jewish emancipation—which went hand in hand with the struggle for a liberal, democratic, secular state—played out over many decades. In England,

Jews faced legal restrictions until 1858. In Germany, Jews had gained full equality only in 1869. Now the rise of antisemitism was threatening those gains. At stake in the Dreyfus Affair therefore was not only the fate of one man who had been wrongly accused, but the fate of democratic systems of government that were remaking the world along more equitable lines. The entire world would soon start watching to see how it played out.

In the fall of 1896, *L'Éclair* made known the existence of the secret file used to convict Dreyfus. But what was still not known—except to the army's top brass—was just how little actual evidence that file contained. Although the newspaper had claimed that one of the messages exchanged between the German and Italian military attachés had named Dreyfus specifically, this was not in fact the case. Perhaps acting on his own or perhaps acting at the suggestion of General Gonse, Commandant Henry therefore decided to fabricate such a document. On the night of Sunday, November 1, 1896, he assembled several letters between Schwarzkoppen and Panizzardi culled from the "ordinary track." Armed with a pen knife and some transparent tape, he cut out bits from the letters and pasted them into a new document, in which he forged the following message in Panizzardi's handwriting: "I have read that a Deputy is to pursue questioning about Dreyfus. If Rome is asked for new explanations, I will say that I never had any relations with the Jew. If they ask you, say the same, for no one must ever know what happened with him."[7]

Henry resembled neither the new type of technocratic officer embodied by Dreyfus, nor the older, more aristocratic model typified by Picquart, Du Paty de Clam, and Esterhazy. Brawny, uneducated, the son of farmers, he was one of the few members of the General Staff who had risen through the ranks. He projected a kind of unsophisticated, can-do toughness that the generals seemed to trust, and he had managed to secure a position in the Statistical Section despite not knowing any foreign languages and having no particular expertise in counterespionage. He certainly was not a skilled forger. Indeed, he failed to notice that the graph paper on which he forged the message had squares that were tinted blue, while the pieces he had assembled from actual letters, including Panizzardi's signature, had squares that were mauve.

Proud of his accomplishment, Henry brought the document to Generals Gonse and De Boisdeffre, claiming to have discovered a damning piece of evidence against Dreyfus. Perhaps seeing through the fraud, the generals congratulated Henry on his discovery, but chose not to show the new letter to Picquart. Instead, they removed Picquart from his post in the Statistical Section. Picquart knew his superiors wanted him out of the way, but he still could not understand why the army seemed bent on covering up the truth of Dreyfus's innocence. If the military's prestige was at stake, wasn't it better to admit their mistake and rectify it? Wouldn't their cover-up turn an embarrassing error into a much worse scandal? Before departing, Picquart took with him many documents pertaining to the Dreyfus case.

Emboldened by the revelation of the secret file, which the army did not seek to deny, Mathieu decided that the time was ripe for the distribution of Bernard Lazare's pamphlet, which the journalist had revised to include the new information that had emerged. *A Judicial Error: The Truth About the Dreyfus Affair* was delivered to all the major journalists in Paris, as well as all the members of the Chamber of Deputies, on November 7 and 8, 1896. It described the contents of the bordereau and revealed that the explosive document alluded to in *L'Éclair* did not actually mention Dreyfus by name, only the letter "D." At this point there was no turning back: Mathieu, who had wanted to work behind the scenes to secure his brother's release, realized that his struggle had to take place in the open. He also realized that his best hope lay in swaying popular opinion in his brother's favor.[8]

Soon there was another major break in the case: on November 10, 1896, the newspaper *Le Matin* published a facsimile of the bordereau, which had been leaked by one of the handwriting experts who examined it during the trial. From this Dreyfus's family could plainly see that he was not the author of the document that had served as the central piece of evidence against him. So too could Schwarzkoppen, the German military attaché, who of course knew that he had had no dealings with Dreyfus. Unlike Dreyfus's family, however, the German also recognized the writing of the bordereau as being in the hand of Esterhazy. He considered coming forward with this information but decided not to for fear of compromising one of his spies.

Henry, who knew Esterhazy from the time when they had worked together in the Statistical Section years before, grew worried that Esterhazy's handwriting would be recognized. On December 14, Henry decided to create a new forgery to allay any doubts about Dreyfus's guilt. The letter, supposedly addressed to Picquart by a mysterious personage named "Speranza," described how Picquart and the "Jewish syndicate" were acting on Dreyfus's behalf. Feigning alarm, Henry showed the document to his superiors. Whether or not they believed in the authenticity of Henry's document, the generals wanted Picquart permanently out of the way since he risked exposing their machinations against Dreyfus. They decided to ship him off on a dangerous mission to Tunisia.

While in Tunisia, Picquart exchanged several letters with Henry, whose insolence convinced him that the General Staff had determined to purge him from their ranks. He requested leave to return to Paris, and on June 20, 1897, he went to see a lawyer, Louis Leblois. Confiding to him his knowledge of Dreyfus's innocence and Esterhazy's guilt, Picquart entrusted to Leblois the files he had removed from his office—in case something should happen to him in Tunisia. Picquart forbade Leblois from communicating with the Dreyfus family but in-

structed him to tell what he knew to the government "if necessary." Once Picquart had departed, Leblois decided to share the
information with the most important government official he
knew, Auguste Scheurer-Kestner.

Scheurer-Kestner was a former deputy from Alsace, a Protestant from a wealthy industrialist family. After the loss of the
province in 1871, instead of losing his seat, he was made a
senator-for-life. By 1897, he was vice president of the Senate
and the last remaining legislator from Alsace. He carried an un-
paralleled moral weight. He had been interested in the Dreyfus
case for several years already, letting it be known that he had
his doubts about the guilt of the Jewish officer from his native
province. Leblois shared with him all the evidence compiled by
Picquart but, in deference to the latter, made Scheurer-Kestner
promise not to reveal what he knew. Loyal to his oath, the Alsatian senator nevertheless instructed his friend Joseph Reinach
to tell Dreyfus's family that he was convinced of his innocence.
Knowing that they had the support of such an august personage buoyed the spirits of Mathieu and Lucie at a crucial time.

Generals de Boisdeffre and Gonse grew alarmed when intelligence reports reached them that Leblois had met first with
Picquart and then with Scheurer-Kestner. They suspected that
Picquart was actively collaborating with the "Jewish syndicate"
to expose Esterhazy as the true culprit. Again, rather than admit
they had convicted the wrong man, the army went further down
the path of cover-up and collusion. Over the course of the fall
and winter 1897, Henry and Du Paty de Clam met frequently
with Esterhazy, attempting to allay his fears of exposure and to
prevent the unstable officer from acting imprudently. Henry,
who had since been promoted to lieutenant colonel, kept forging
documents to incriminate Dreyfus and even bragged to Maurice
Paléologue, a diplomat in the ministry of foreign affairs, that he
had a "closet full" of evidence against the Jewish soldier.[9]

It was at this point that more French people began to take

an interest in the case. In his *Souvenirs sur l'Affaire*, Léon Blum recounts how he was just finishing his summer vacation in 1897 when the librarian at the École normale supérieure, Lucien Herr, came to see him in the countryside outside of Paris. "Did you know that Dreyfus is innocent?" he asked. Blum recalled the case of the Jewish officer who had been condemned for espionage three years before, an unpleasant episode that Jewish families like his had attempted to forget. Herr soon brought him up to speed on the case, telling him about Bernard Lazare's pamphlet, the secret dossier, and the bordereau. Blum was flabbergasted. Quickly, the affair came to occupy his every waking moment, as it would for so many young people of his generation. As Blum puts it, "The Affair was a human crisis, less drawn out and less prolonged but just as violent as the French Revolution and the Great War."[10]

During the fall and winter of 1897, the small band of Dreyfus supporters began to swell. Herr hosted meetings at his home in the Latin Quarter of fellow academics, students, and former students who were united in recognizing in the Dreyfus case a test of democratic principles and a sign of the overreaching power of the military in French national life. They in turn fanned out through Paris, attempting to interest more people in the case. Blum went to see the writer Maurice Barrès, a hero to left-leaning youth for his popular trilogy *The Cult of the Self*, which vaunted the pleasure of the senses. Barrès rebuffed him—he would go on to embrace nationalism and become one of the most vehement anti-Dreyfusards.

Then, on November 7, 1897, a stockbroker named J. de Castro happened to see one of the facsimiles of the bordereau that Mathieu Dreyfus had distributed around Paris. He recognized the handwriting of his client, Esterhazy. De Castro arranged for a meeting with Mathieu and showed him examples of Esterhazy's handwriting. This was the break Mathieu had been waiting for. Armed with the identity of the real culprit, Dreyfus's brother went to see Scheurer-Kestner, who had sworn not to reveal the truth about Esterhazy to the Dreyfus family. But once the family had independently learned the truth, the senator no longer felt obligated to maintain the secret. He shared with Mathieu the information that Picquart had entrusted to his lawyer Leblois. Mathieu was shocked to learn that the General Staff had known for months of Esterhazy's guilt, and hence of his brother's innocence, but had kept silent.

On December 15, 1897, Mathieu published a letter to the minister of war exposing Esterhazy as the author of the bordereau. Backed into a corner, the army announced that it would launch another investigation into the case. With his role as a spy plainly exposed, Esterhazy went rogue, giving interviews to various Parisian dailies in which he made preposterous claims, including that Dreyfus had traced his handwriting when he wrote the bordereau. He also blamed the Jews for organizing a conspiracy against him.

Ruth Harris has recently complicated our understanding of the neat division between the two sides in the affair by showing, among other things, that not all of the anti-Dreyfusards were antisemites and that there were in fact some antisemites in the pro-Dreyfus camp. To be sure, there was much more at stake in the case than antisemitism. And some of those who became passionate supporters of Dreyfus may have at one time harbored negative views of Jews. But just as antisemitism had become a "cultural code" expressing a range of right-wing political opinions, so too had opposition to Dreyfus come to signify a largely overlapping set of beliefs, including religious conservatism and anti-republican authoritarianism. And on the flip side, advocacy on behalf of Dreyfus became a way of registering support for the liberal democratic republic.[11]

No one among these new converts to the Dreyfusard cause was more significant than the novelist Émile Zola, who himself had expressed negative opinions of Jews in the past (for instance,

in his novel *L'Argent* (Money) in 1890, he described the area
around the Paris Stock Exchange as "a whole filthy Jewish quarter . . . an extraordinary meeting of characteristic noses [*toute
une juiverie malpropre . . . une extraordinaire réunion de nez typ-
iques*]").[12] But outraged by Drumont's provocations and awak-
ened to the threat the campaign against the Jews posed to the
republic, Zola had referred to it as "a monstrosity" in an article
published in *Le Figaro* in 1896. No doubt because of this article, the partisans of Dreyfus—including Lazare and Scheurer-
Kestner—approached Zola and persuaded him to write more
articles in support of their cause. In "The Record [*Procès-verbal*],"
published in *Le Figaro* on December 5, 1897, Zola denounced
"the poison of antisemitism" once again. And in his "Letter to
the Youth," he urged the young generation to fight for the cause
of truth and justice. Other centrist and left-leaning journalists
also joined the Dreyfusard effort at this point, including Yves
Guyot, whose pointed interventions in *Le Siècle* were picked up
by newspapers around the world. Georges Clemenceau, the future prime minister, began to wage his own campaign on behalf
of Dreyfus in his newspaper *L'Aurore*.

It would take a while, however, for French Socialists to join
the Dreyfusard cause. Jean Jaurès, the Socialist leader who had
attended the École polytechnique at the same time as Dreyfus,
at first believed that the case did not concern the working class.
It would be one thing, he wrote in *La Petite république* on December 11, 1897, if the accused had been a "poor man," without
money and relations. But Socialists did not have to take up arms
to defend a well-connected military officer and a capitalist like
Dreyfus. Even while denouncing the way that Dreyfus had been
sentenced based on secret evidence as "the crime of crimes,"
Jaurès, like his fellow Socialist Jules Guesde, who led the orthodox Marxist wing of the party, at first saw the case as a conflict
between two factions of the privileged class—Jews and Protestants on one side and Catholics and the military on the other.

The Socialist association of Jews with the capitalist enemy drew on a long-standing tradition of left-wing antisemitism, one that Drumont had astutely tapped in *La France juive*.[13]

When Jaurès eventually rallied to the Dreyfusard cause, it had a profound effect. Addressing the Chamber of Deputies on January 24, 1898, the Socialist leader defended "every citizen's right to protection" by the laws of the nation and denounced antisemitic prejudice as a danger to the republic. "Towards a Jew as towards any other person," he declared, "we have the right to demand that legal guarantees be observed."[14] Later that year, Jaurès published a volume entitled *Les Preuves* (The Proof), laying out the facts of the case with remarkable precision and characterizing Dreyfus, the Jewish soldier, as "nothing more than humanity itself at the lowest imaginable point of misery and despair."[15] The result was a split within the Socialist ranks. Although the followers of Guesde would continue to keep their distance because Dreyfus was a wealthy Jew, Jaurès helped ensure that a large part of the political left in France would align itself with republican values and against antisemitism for decades to come.[16]

On January 1, 1898, the military authorities announced that Esterhazy would be court-martialed for espionage. The supporters of Dreyfus hoped that the truth would finally come to light. But even while gesturing toward justice, the generals in charge decided that military witnesses would be questioned in secret to ensure that the press would not hear Picquart's damning evidence. After a short, two-day trial on January 10–11, the judges deliberated for all of three minutes before acquitting Esterhazy unanimously. The military now had not only condemned a man it knew to be innocent but had absolved a man it knew to be a spy.

Applause broke out in the courtroom, along with chants of "Long live France!" "Death to the Jews!" and "Death to the syndicate!" A crowd of more than a thousand people met Esterhazy as he exited the building a free man, and someone shouted, "Hats off to the martyr of the Jews." *La Libre parole* exulted: "Any Yid who, to his misfortune, might pass by, would be lynched without fail. Canes wave, fists clench. Long live the army! Down with the Jews."[17] The right-wing daily *L'Echo de Paris* referred to the verdict as a "relief" and admonished, "It was a great error on the part of the Jewish world to have appeared to make common cause with Dreyfus."[18] The next day, Picquart was put in prison and Scheurer-Kestner stripped of his position as vice president of the Senate. Crowds in front of the Moulin Rouge burned an effigy of Mathieu Dreyfus in front of a makeshift gallows.[19]

The verdict in the Esterhazy trial did not take Zola by surprise. Convinced that the only way forward lay in exposing the affair to as wide a public as possible, he resolved to publish an article summarizing the dark machinations of the military authorities in the cases of Dreyfus and Esterhazy. After two nights of feverish composition, he brought the text to Clemenceau's newspaper *L'Aurore* because *Le Figaro*, where he had published his earlier articles in defense of Dreyfus, had turned anti-Dreyfusard. Titled "Letter to the President of the Republic," the article bore the banner headline "J'Accuse . . . !"—*I accuse*. On the morning of January 13, 1898, newsboys screamed the phrase in the streets, quickly selling out the entire print run of 300,000 copies.

A rhetorical masterpiece, Zola's article compared the twists and turns of the case to the plot of a lowbrow novel and concluded with the famous phrase "J'Accuse" repeated over and over to denounce the miscarriage of justice and the cover-up that followed. "I accuse Lt. Col. du Paty de Clam of being the diabolical creator of this miscarriage of justice," Zola began, before training his sights—and his scorn—on the minister of war: "I accuse General Mercier of complicity, at least by mental weakness, in one of the greatest inequities of the century." Zola did not spare the mendacious journalists on the right, either: "I accuse the War Office of using the press, particularly *L'Eclair* and *L'Echo de Paris*, to conduct an abominable campaign to mislead the general public and cover up their own wrongdoing." And he concluded by indicting the judges in the trials of both Dreyfus and Esterhazy: "Finally, I accuse the first court-martial of violating the law by convicting the accused on the basis of a document that was kept secret, and I accuse the second court-martial of covering up this illegality, on orders, thus committing the judicial crime of knowingly acquitting a guilty man."

Although Zola hoped that the public might be swayed by his accusations, he had another goal in mind as well. By openly accusing high-ranking members of the military of conspiracy and cover-up, he was forcing them to sue him for libel. And since libel was a civil crime, the case would have to be heard by a civil—rather than a military—court, which meant that the military would no longer be able to keep the evidence a secret. "The action I am taking," Zola wrote at the end of "J'Accuse," "is no more than a radical measure to hasten the explosion of truth and justice." Scheurer-Kestner thought he had gone too far. But Zola believed that nothing less than a public accusation of the leading conspirators, even one that was sure to result in his own prosecution, was needed to bring the truth to light. It was a stunning gambit for a successful novelist who had a tremendous amount to lose.

At the time "J'Accuse" hit the newsstands on January 13, 1898, most people in France still believed Dreyfus to be guilty. This was not, or not only, because of antisemitism, but because definitive proof of his innocence had not yet come to light. Although it was now known that the handwriting of the bordereau was not that of Dreyfus, it was not yet widely known how little actual evidence the army had against the Jewish officer. The judges at the trials of both Dreyfus and Esterhazy had reached unanimous verdicts, and no precedent existed for questioning the authority of military courts. Even people of good will had difficulty believing that the army they so revered could have knowingly sent an innocent man to prison and engaged in a massive cover-up to protect an enemy spy. And yet, antisemitism was undeniably the cause of the vast mobilization against Dreyfus that took place in the days and weeks following the publication of "J'Accuse."[20]

Zola's article generated an enormous backlash against Jews, a public demonstration of hatred the likes of which France had never seen. The extent of the anti-Jewish antipathy is shocking. Over the course of several months, no fewer than sixty-nine cities and towns in metropolitan France and colonial Algeria—including many locales with few or no Jews—witnessed anti-Jewish agitation that can be compared to the pogroms that shook the Russian empire during the 1880s, even if there were fewer fatalities. According to Pierre Birnbaum, "French society, both openly and covertly, abandoned itself in great measure to a multiform anti-Semitism."[21]

The first demonstrations occurred in Paris on the day after the publication of "J'Accuse." They were led by Catholic students shouting "Out with Scheurer! Out with Zola! Down with the Jews!" Although antisemitism was not the only factor motivating the rioters, it was certainly a major one. In his coverage of the event, Drumont made sure to emphasize the anti-Jewish element: "Like scalded rats, the Jews no longer know which way to turn," he crowed in *La Libre parole*.[22] And as the riot spilled over to the *grands boulevards* and to streets throughout the capital, the demonstrators—a heterogeneous group that came to include students, apprentices, and salaried workers—threw stones at the windows of businesses they believed to be owned by Jews. Taking advantage of the ferment, Drumont and the nationalist leader Henri Rochefort organized a mass political meeting at Tivoli Hall on January 17 to protest the "machinations of international Jewry and its accomplices intended to dishonor France." The right-wing newspaper *L'Intransigeant* estimated that eight thousand people attended. Protests continued to build over the next week, with posters calling for a mass demonstration on January 23, 1898, against "the organizers of treason, the accomplices of cosmopolitan Jewry." Thousands attended once again, shouting, "Out with Zola! Death to the Jews! Death to the Yids! Long live the army!"[23]

As Paris continued to smolder, unrest spread to the provinces. In Lyon, Grenoble, and cities and towns throughout the French heartland, protesters marched against the Jews and their accomplice, Zola. In Nancy, protesters destroyed Jewish-owned shops and besieged the synagogue. In Rennes, a crowd of two thousand attacked the homes of prominent Jewish professors. In Lyon and Bordeaux, rioters broke windows of the Nouvelles Galeries, a department store belonging to Jews. Similar scenes played out in all the major cities of France: Marseilles, Montpellier, Angoulême, Grenoble, Lille, Rouen, Angers, Caen, Nantes, Tours, Poitiers, and Toulouse.[24]

The worst violence occurred in colonial Algeria. Ever since 1870, when the nascent Third Republic had naturalized Algeria's more than thirty thousand Jews, anti-Jewish sentiment had been building, mainly among the European population of the colony. The Dreyfus Affair brought tensions to a crisis point. Rioters pillaged Jewish stores and ransacked synagogues in May 1897. After Zola launched his "bomb" in January 1898, bloody anti-Jewish demonstrations broke out in the major cities of Algeria. Christian shop owners put up signs proclaiming they were not Jewish to avoid the destruction. Rioters burned Zola in effigy. On January 23, 1898, Jews were stoned and beaten in the street. Several died, including some policemen; hundreds were injured, and hundreds more were arrested. Over the course of 1898, anti-Jewish riots occurred on an almost a daily basis throughout Algeria.[25]

It was in Algeria, moreover, that antisemitism mutated into a potent political force. Max Régis, a charismatic rabblerouser, founded an antisemitic newspaper, *L'Antijuif* (The Anti-Jew), in Algiers in 1897, modeled on *La Libre parole*. During the riots following the publication of "J'Accuse," Régis declared, "We will water the tree of liberty with the blood of Jews." His followers formed paramilitary bands and regularly marched through the streets singing: "Death to the Jews! Death to the Jews! We must hang them without further ado." Régis promoted the candidacy of his idol Drumont for the legislative assembly from second ward of Algiers in February 1898. Drumont won easily, despite not living in Algeria, and together with three other deputies from Algiers he founded the "antisemitic caucus" in the Chamber. Régis himself was elected mayor of Algiers in November 1898 and proceeded to enact discriminatory legislation against Jewish citizens before being removed from his post in 1899 by the governor-general for insulting government authorities.[26]

Yet more than a few historians have asserted that antisemitism was peripheral to the Dreyfus Affair. Guy Chapman's widely read English-language account in 1955 declared that "there was little substantial antisemitism" in France at the time of the affair, and that Jew-hatred was confined to Parisian high society. Although Chapman acknowledged the antisemitic riots of 1898, he dismissed them as mere troublemaking by ne'er-do-wells.[27] Chapman may represent an extreme case, but some of the leading French historians today continue to downplay the importance of antisemitism to the affair. Bertrand Joly, for example, grudgingly admits that "antisemitism, which was marginal in 1890, began to make a certain echo in society" during the affair, but suggests that attributing to it anything more than a marginal place would constitute an anachronism. Joly also questions to what extent the riots in 1898 were in fact motivated by antisemitism. Although he admits that the rioters always chanted antisemitic slogans, he maintains that it was nationalist and patriotic sentiment, and not anti-Jewish anger, that was the main driver of unrest. "It is extremely probable," he writes, "that for the majority of French people in 1898, the 'Jewish question' signified absolutely nothing."[28]

But if many French people, especially in rural areas, did not know Jews personally, they were certainly aware of the violent antisemitic riots throughout France. And as Nancy Fitch has shown, organized political antisemitism did invade the French countryside during the affair. In the elections of 1898, which followed the antisemitic riots, twenty-two openly antisemitic candidates were elected to the Chamber of Deputies. Only five of these represented urban districts.

Birnbaum makes it clear, however, that although antisemites pushed French institutions to the breaking point in 1898, these institutions did not ultimately break. Many courageous individuals stood up for justice. Joseph Reinach, the Jewish deputy representing the Basses-Alpes region, refused to keep silent about the affair, even though he knew that speaking out on behalf of Dreyfus endangered his seat. "To know that an illegality, that a judicial error has been committed, and to keep quiet, is to make oneself complicit," he proclaimed in a statement of his beliefs issued in advance of the election. Reinach went on to lose the election of 1898, but he regained his seat in 1906, the year that Dreyfus was finally exonerated.[29] Zola's incendiary article opened the eyes of many others who until then had hesitated to express an opinion on an obscure and confusing juridical matter. At the height of the affair, Lucie Dreyfus received more than a thousand letters a day from well-wishers from throughout France and around the world.[30]

On January 15, 1898, immediately after the publication of "J'Accuse," Zola and several associates launched the first petition demanding a revision of the verdict against Dreyfus and gathered the signatures of prominent academics, scientists, lawyers, and doctors, as well as writers such as Anatole France and Marcel Proust, many of whom had never before taken a stand on political issues. The painter Claude Monet added his name to the list in the following days, as did the sociologist Émile Durkheim, and many other famous figures—some Jewish, some not. Clemenceau published the petition on January 14, 1898, in *L'Aurore* under the heading, "Manifesto of the Intellectuals." The modern use of the term "intellectual" to refer to members of the cultural vanguard who intervene in political matters to challenge the status quo dates from this moment in the affair. It remains one of the major contributions of the affair to French cultural life.[31]

On February 24, 1898, Dreyfusard intellectuals founded the League of the Rights of Man to mobilize support for the Jewish officer. They were countered by the anti-Dreyfusard League of the French Fatherland, which also counted prominent writers—including Maurice Barrès and Jules Verne—among its members. Behind these two leagues lay two opposing conceptions of French society. The Dreyfusards shared a liberal, pluralistic vision of the nation, in which the rights of the individual were paramount, and Jews and other minorities would enjoy full equality. They opposed the influence of the Catholic Church in French life and sought to reduce the political power of the military. The anti-Dreyfusards, in contrast, embraced a deterministic model of French identity defined by race and religion, which excluded Jews—even those Jews, like Dreyfus, whose families had lived in France for centuries. The motto of *La Libre parole*—"France for the French"—summarized their views. They were nostalgic for a time when traditional Catholic values held sway and immoral practices like divorce—made legal thanks to the efforts of the Jewish deputy Alfred-Joseph Naquet—were banned. Many anti-Dreyfusards opposed democracy altogether and openly advocated for a return to monarchy.[32]

Over the course of the next two years, French society—or at least the society in French towns and cities—broke in two because of the affair. Many prominent and up-and-coming writers were Dreyfusard, including Zola, Anatole France, Marcel Proust, Charles Péguy, and André Gide. Other writers were militantly anti-Dreyfusard, including Gyp (pseudonym of Sybille Riquetti de Mirabeau), Paul Valéry, Paul Bourget, and Léon Daudet, along with Barrès and Verne.[33] Even the Impressionists were divided: Monet, Camille Pissarro, Paul Signac, and Mary Cassatt were Dreyfusard; Paul Cézanne, Auguste Rodin, Pierre-Auguste Renoir, and Edgar Degas were anti-Dreyfusard. Proust provides one of the most penetrating accounts of this polarization in his epic masterpiece *À la Recherche du temps perdu* (*In Search of Lost Time*, 1913–1927), which describes how Parisian drawing rooms became the battlegrounds of the affair. One of Proust's main concerns is to show how the political animosities unleashed by the affair led to deep divisions in all classes as well as within families, as opinions about Dreyfus divided parents from their children, husbands from their wives. Proust's own family was similarly divided: he and his brother sided with their Jewish mother in support of Dreyfus, while his non-Jewish father, a prominent doctor, took up the cause of the army.[34]

At Zola's libel trial in February 1898, one military officer after another—General Mercier, General de Boisdeffre, General Gonse, Commandant du Paty de Clam, Colonel Henry—testified to Dreyfus's guilt. When pressed about the existence of the secret dossier, Mercier refused to respond. The graphologist Bertillon gave a befuddled account of how the bordereau was written by Dreyfus even though the handwriting was so different, provoking laughter in the courtroom. As Esterhazy watched the proceedings, he grew increasingly enraged, predicting that if Dreyfus were to set foot in France again, "there would be 5,000 Jewish corpses in the streets of Paris." When he finally took the stand, he refused to answer questions about his relations with Schwarzkoppen.[35]

The imprisoned Picquart gave dramatic testimony. Responding to Henry's open accusation in the courtroom that he had lied, he threw caution to the wind, declaring:

> Gentlemen of the jury, it has now been I don't know how much time, months that I have been heaped with insults by newspapers that are paid to spread such slander and untruth. ... For months, I remained in the situation most horrible for an officer, since my honor was attacked and I was unable to defend myself! Tomorrow, perhaps, I will be expelled from the Army that I love and to which I have given twenty-five years of my life! That did not stop me, when I thought it my duty to pursue truth and justice. I did so, and in so doing I believed I was rending a greater service to my country and to the Army. It was thus that I believed it incumbent upon me to perform my duty as an honest man.[36]

Picquart went on to give detailed and credible testimony describing how Esterhazy had access to all the information in the bordereau. It seemed to most observers that he had swayed the jury and that Zola would be found innocent of libel.

In a desperate move to counter the impression made by Picquart, General Georges de Pellieux then took the stand and unveiled what he believed was a secret weapon: the document naming Dreyfus that had been forged by Henry. Until this point, Generals de Boisdeffre and Gonse had merely alluded to the existence of this document, which they knew to be fake. Pellieux had committed a colossal blunder by describing it in detail. The other generals rushed to cover for him, arguing that reasons of state security prevented them from showing the document in court. They guaranteed its authenticity. This was enough for the jury, which delivered the verdict: Zola was guilty of libel.

However, Zola had succeeded in his aim of shedding light on the paucity of real evidence used to convict Dreyfus. The Dreyfusards now had more information about the documents that they knew must be false. They scored a minor victory when the High Court of Appeal overturned the verdict against Zola, forcing another trial. In the meantime, legislative elections led to the fall of the government, largely in response to the agitation over the affair. Upon taking office, Godefroy Cavaignac, the new minister of war who was known to be anti-Dreyfusard, asked to examine the secret file used to condemn Dreyfus. In a dramatic speech before the Chamber of Deputies on July 7, 1898, he detailed the contents of the file, implicitly guaranteeing the authenticity of the documents. He was greeted with acclamations by the deputies who wanted to put the affair behind them.

Since the generals knew that the accusations made against them by Zola in "J'Accuse" were largely correct, they had wisely chosen to focus their prosecution for libel on a single sentence in which Zola had alleged that the military judges had acquitted Esterhazy "on command." They knew this would be difficult for Zola to prove. When the government declared that Zola would not be allowed to present evidence in support of his other claims at his second trial, the Dreyfusards persuaded the novelist to flee to England rather than receive another guilty verdict. Zola was found guilty a second time and sentenced to prison *in absentia*.

The Dreyfusards now knew that a secret file had been shared with Dreyfus's judges, in violation of the law, and that it contained obviously fake documents. However, they could not prove their allegations so long as the generals continued to stonewall by refusing to present the documents for examination by Dreyfus's lawyers. Then, on the evening of August 13, 1898, Cavaignac ordered Captain Louis Cuignet to reexamine the items in the secret file. The minister was opposed to Dreyfus and was hoping that this review would reveal damning evidence. Instead, Cuignet noticed that the document naming Dreyfus was composed on graph paper of differing colors—an obvious forgery by Henry. He brought his findings to Cavaignac, who despite his political leanings, decided he could not hide the truth.

On August 30, Colonel Henry was summoned to appear before Cavaignac. In the presence of De Boisdeffre and Gonse, he confessed to the forgery. That night, in prison, Henry wrote a letter to his wife deflecting blame: "You know in whose interest I acted," he wrote. The next morning, the guards found him dead in his cell. He had slit his own throat.

The revelation of the forgeries and Henry's suicide marked a definitive turning point in the affair. On October 29, 1898, the Criminal Chamber of the High Court of Appeal granted Lucie Dreyfus's request for an appeal of her husband's verdict. In the months that followed, France underwent still more political instability linked to the affair. Despite having uncovered proof of Dreyfus's innocence, Cavaignac remained a committed anti-Dreyfusard and resigned from the ministry rather than preside over the next stage of the affair, when the verdict against Dreyfus would surely be overturned.

Meanwhile, shocking events brought France closer to political crisis. On February 16, 1899, French president Félix Faure, who had long opposed the revision of the verdict against Dreyfus, died of apoplexy while having sex with his mistress in the Élysée Palace. He was replaced by Émile Loubet, who was seen as more sympathetic to the Dreyfusards. This infuriated the far right. On the day of Faure's funeral, the popular anti-Dreyfusard deputy Paul Déroulède attempted a coup but failed to persuade government troops to march on the Élysée. He stood trial in May and, despite promising openly that he would attempt another coup should he be set free, was acquitted by a sympathetic jury.

On June 3, 1899, after deliberating for two days, the High Court of Appeal found that there had been insufficient evidence to convict Dreyfus in 1894 and overturned the guilty verdict.[37]

This was not equivalent to exoneration, but it was a first step in that direction. No longer considered a criminal, merely an accused man, the prisoner of Devil's Island would return to France to face a new military court-martial, this time in the provincial city of Rennes. Zola took this as a cue to return to France and request a new trial for himself as well. The military then released Picquart from prison and dropped all charges against him. The last act of the affair had begun.

5

───◆◦◆◦◆───

The Climax

WHILE FRANCE DEVOLVED into a kind of civil war because of the affair, Dreyfus engaged in a solitary struggle for survival on Devil's Island. Along with the dreaded "double buckle," which bound him to the bed, the guards imposed other tortures as security measures, including a light burning above his bed at night, which attracted insects and prevented him from sleeping. In the fall of 1896, they surrounded his hut with two high perimeter walls that blocked his view of the sea. After months of confinement to his hut while the construction took place, Dreyfus was finally allowed to walk inside the encircled area, although no shade protected him from the burning sun.[1]

In August 1897, the prison authorities moved him to a newly built hut on a different part of the island. The new hut was divided in two by an iron grill, with Dreyfus on one side and guards on the other, watching his every move. He suffered from recurrent bouts of fever and parasite-borne illnesses. As his health declined, the authorities discussed what to do in the event of his death. The director of the prison in Cayenne, the capital of French Guiana, sent the commander on the Salvation Islands the materials necessary to embalm his body and ship it back to France. Their main concern was proving that he had not escaped. "So that the face remains completely intact, the brain should be left within the cranium," they instructed.[2]

Dreyfus was not a religious man, but in the depth of his despair, he sought guidance from a higher power. One night in 1897, chained to his bed, with bugs crawling over his head and body, he looked for what he termed a "guiding star," and heard his path forward dictated to him by a voice within: "Today, less than ever, do you have the right to desert your post," he heard the voice say. "Whatever tortures they inflict on you, you must march forward until they throw you in the tomb, you must remain upright before your executioners as long as you have the slightest force."[3] From that moment, he made the resolution to resist more energetically than before. "It is not only a question of my life," he wrote to Lucie, "it is a question of my honor."[4]

News reports from France reached him months delayed, if at all. In September 1897, he received a letter from Lucie, dated July 15, referring to a development that she had supposedly mentioned in a previous letter: "I have been less anguished and the future has finally appeared to me in less somber colors," she wrote. Lucie was no doubt referring to having learned that Scheurer-Kestner believed in Dreyfus's innocence. However, since Dreyfus had not received her earlier letter, he did not understand the hopeful allusion. Even if he had received the earlier letter, he would probably not have understood, since Lucie's letters were so heavily censored by the authorities. He remained in complete ignorance of Esterhazy's trial, Zola's "J'Accuse," the antisemitic riots, the revelation of Henry's forgery, and Henry's suicide.[5]

On October 27, 1898, Dreyfus received word that he would

soon receive a response to his request for a revision of the judgment against him. He had no idea that a request for revision
had been made on his behalf. In November 1898, he received a
letter from Lucie announcing that the request had been accepted,
later confirmed by an official telegram from the commander of
the prison. He described feeling an immense sense of relief as
he began to see his exoneration on the horizon. He had never
doubted that the truth would come to light, only whether he
would live to see it. That winter, he was able to read the revision
request and learned for the first time of Esterhazy's treachery.
From this he realized that the army had not only framed him
but had actively engaged in a cover-up to protect a guilty man.[6]

On June 5, 1899, at 12:30 P.M., the chief guard entered his
hut and presented Dreyfus with a note announcing that the
verdict against him had been overturned. "By virtue of this decree, Captain Dreyfus ceases to be subject to deportation." Restored to his rank and allowed to don his uniform once again,
Dreyfus would return to France to face a new court-martial at
Rennes. "My joy was immense, unspeakable," he wrote. "After
the Court's decree, I believed that the end was now in sight, that
there now remained only a simple formality."[7]

Newspapers around the world covered Dreyfus's return to
France. "A shif aroysgeshikt tsu breyngen Dreyfus [A ship sent
to fetch Dreyfus]" rejoiced the Yiddish daily *Forverts* (Forward)
on June 1, 1899. On June 9, the front page of the *New York Times*
announced that a dispatch boat called the *Goeland* had left the
harbor in Cayenne to transfer the prisoner from Devil's Island
to the *Sfax*, the cruiser that would carry him across the Atlantic.
Still considered a prisoner, Dreyfus was permitted to walk on
the deck of the *Sfax* for one hour in the morning and one hour
in the evening during the three-week journey. The rest of the
time he was confined to his cabin, which in spite of the bars on
its porthole felt extremely luxurious compared with the conditions he had known for almost five years. He resolved to main-

tain his dignity aboard the ship. For an intensely private man like Dreyfus, this meant speaking to the other officers only when strictly necessary.[8]

On June 30, the coast of France came into view. "After five years of martyrdom, I had returned to seek justice. The horrible nightmare was coming to an end," he wrote. "I expected to see my loved ones and behind them, my comrades waiting for me with open arms, tears in their eyes." Disillusionment came quickly. His debarkation at the port of Quiberon, in western Brittany, took place under cover of darkness and a heavy police presence. He began to understand that the French public still viewed him as a traitor. "Fortunately, the long and sad months of captivity had taught me how to steel my emotions, my nerves, and my body with an immense force of resistance," he wrote.[9]

The reunion with Lucie took place the next day, on July 1, 1899. Despite his efforts to remain calm, Dreyfus shook violently and the tears that he had repressed for five years finally began to flow. He experienced similar emotion when he embraced his brother Mathieu, who found him greatly aged by his ordeal, even though he was still not yet forty years old. At that first meeting, watched by a guard, Lucie did not dare discuss his case. However, over the course of the next week, Dreyfus received visits in prison from his lawyers. For the second courtmartial, Mathieu had engaged not just the highly respected Edgar Demange, who had represented Dreyfus at the first courtmartial, but also a brilliant young lawyer, Fernand Labori, who had a more aggressive and confrontational manner. They acquainted their client with all the twists and turns of the affair. Despite suffering from continual bouts of fever, Dreyfus studied the transcripts of his trial from 1894, along with the transcripts of the Esterhazy and Zola trials, in preparation for his testimony. The lawyers confirmed his dawning fear that despite the lack of credible evidence against him, vindication was far from assured.

Dreyfus began to understand that what had once seemed a purely legal matter had become a political one. Even though proof of the conspiracy against him and of the cover-up to protect Esterhazy had come to light, the military still refused to acknowledge the facts. And millions of French people remained wedded to a lie. "We cannot explain how . . . a considerable fraction of the public has remained stubbornly resistant to all the revelations that have emerged in the past year," declared the Jewish newspaper *L'Univers israélite*.[10] Likewise, in *Souvenirs sur l'Affaire*, Léon Blum marveled that anyone could refuse to believe what was so clearly the truth of the case. "How could they not accept Dreyfus's innocence?" he asked. "How could sincere people be anti-Dreyfusards?"[11]

By the time of Dreyfus's second trial at Rennes, there were, in fact, several different types of anti-Dreyfusards. The first were the "sincere" anti-Dreyfusards: those who trusted that the military had acted in good faith and believed in the principle of *res judicata*—a matter that had been decided should not be relitigated. As Bertrand Joly argues, these people were not necessarily wicked or stupid. They were not in favor of keeping an innocent man in prison, even a Jew, but they could not fathom that so many prominent government officials had lied about his guilt. They may have had some doubts, but in the absence of concrete proof of Dreyfus's innocence, they chose to trust the declarations of five successive ministers of war that he was guilty.[12]

The next group of anti-Dreyfusards consisted of those who had something to gain from a second conviction. This category included all of the military officers involved in the collusion and cover-up. It also included those who had not actively colluded, but who had staked their reputations on affirming Dreyfus's guilt. In this category could be placed the right-wing politicians and writers whose popularity soared thanks to their involvement in the case, such as the journalist Édouard Drumont and the writer Maurice Barrès, whose novel *Les Déracinés* (The Uprooted, 1897) celebrated the cult of militarism and popularized xenophobic nationalism.[13]

Writers such as Drumont and Barrès were largely responsible for enflaming the passions of the third category of anti-Dreyfusards—the antisemites, those less interested in the facts of the case than in punishing Dreyfus for what they believed were the sins of the Jews. This collection included the people who formed mobs after the publication of "J'Accuse," but it also included a surprising number of law-abiding citizens who burned with quiet rage toward the Jewish minority that constituted less than two-tenths of a percent of the French population. The affair focused their hatred and liberated it from constraints.

Since the real target of the antisemites' wrath was not Dreyfus himself but Jews in general, they were not dissuaded when the case against Dreyfus fell apart. If anything, they grew more strident in their desire to punish the Jewish traitor and the "Jewish syndicate" *after* it appeared that Dreyfus was innocent. Following Henry's suicide, Drumont began a campaign to raise money for his "widow and orphan" in *La Libre parole*. The stated goal was to defend the honor of the "French officer killed, murdered by the Jews."[14] Within a month, more than twenty-five thousand people had contributed to the so-called Henry Monument, raising more than 130,000 francs.[15] Many of the contributions came with commentaries published by *La Libre parole* that reveal the extent to which the contributors were motivated by antisemitism. The commentaries also reveal the dark, irrational passions underlying this hatred. One priest prayed he might have a "bedside carpet made of kikeskin" so that he could step on it morning and night. A physician proposed "vivisection of Jews rather than harmless rabbits."[16]

Many of the contributions came from workers and craftsmen in industries, such as clothing manufacturing, which had been "invaded" by Jewish immigrants. Other contributions came from working people who felt humiliated by Jewish financial power more generally: "Jeanne, ex-maid for kikes," "a concierge for Jews who is disgusted by kikes," "Three embroiderers of Bains-les-Bains (Vosges), who, working for a Jew, earn 14 sous in 15 hours," "a laborer without work." As Stephen Wilson, a scholar of antisemitism, explains, the Henry Monument served as a kind of collective ritual that compensated for feelings of deprivation and anger at the capitalist system. Not all the contributions, however, came from the lower classes. The liberal professions (doctors, lawyers, teachers) supplied 8.25 percent of the contributions, and students supplied 8.6 percent. There were 4,500 donors from the military, including twenty-eight retired generals. Jean-Denis Bredin counts 433 names bearing the aristocratic particule ("de"), and 336 members of the titled nobility, including seven dukes and duchesses, two princes, and hundreds of counts, viscounts, and barons. For these better-off contributors, antisemitism served as a means of registering hostility not just to capitalism but to the forces of social change or modernity more generally.[17]

A disturbingly large number of the contributions came attached to messages calling for physical violence against Jews. "Long live the saber that will rid us of all the vermin." "A patriot awaiting the saber to avenge us." "For God, for his country and the extermination of the Jews." "The flood of insults against the Army will be washed away in rivers of blood." Some of the messages eerily presaged the Holocaust. One contributor gave 25 centimes, one quarter of a franc, "to rent a deportation car." A resident of Baccarat, the capital of crystal manufacturing, wanted to see "all the kikes and kikettes and their kiddy-kikes placed in glass furnaces."[18] Although Wilson argues that the violence expressed in the Henry Monument remained purely symbolic, it seems clear that it unleashed the imagination of genocide, if not its actual implementation.[19]

These fantasies of extermination were fed by a dehumanizing brand of antisemitic propaganda, and especially by the anti-

semitic images—cartoons, posters, photographs—that prolifer-
ated in fin-de-siècle France thanks to new printing technologies.
One particularly notorious series of posters that appeared during
the affair, titled the Museum of Horrors, featured realistically
drawn heads of prominent Jews attached to grotesque animal
bodies. Dreyfus's head figured on the body of a serpent. Joseph
Reinach, the Dreyfusard politician, took the form of an ape.
Various members of the Rothschild family appeared as hairy
beasts, their claws clutching bags of money, even though they
for the most part had played no public role in the affair. The
series also represented non-Jewish Dreyfusards, including Zola
as a hog, Picquart as a camel, and leading republican politicians
such as Émile Loubet as a trained bear.[20]

The amalgamation of antisemitism and anti-republicanism
peaked during the affair, when the myth of the "Jewish Republic," which is to say a republic dominated by Jews, galvanized
opposition groups from across the political spectrum. Most of
these anti-republicans fit into one of the three other categories
of anti-Dreyfusard described above, but they might also be said
to constitute a fourth category. Their opposition to Dreyfus's
rehabilitation was primarily political and aimed at destabilizing
the republican regime. Paul Déroulède, the nationalist deputy
who had attempted a coup after the funeral of President Faure
in February 1899, openly declared his intention to lead another
coup that summer, as Dreyfus made his way back to France.
Déroulède was eventually arrested for conspiring against the
republic and banished from France for ten years.[21]

Alarmed by these threats, President Loubet called on Pierre
Waldeck-Rousseau, a moderate center-left politician, to form a
cabinet on June 22, 1899. His so-called government of republican defense united disparate political factions—including General Gaston de Galliffet, a conservative who had led the bloody
suppression of the Paris Commune in 1871, and the progres-
sive Socialist leader Alexandre Millerand. Recognizing that the

Museum of Horrors, No. 6: The Traitor! (Imp. Lenepveu, 1899)

Dreyfus case was fueling the anti-republican opposition, Waldeck-Rousseau resolved to liquidate the affair as quickly as possible. Denounced as the "Dreyfus Ministry" in the pages of *La Libre parole*, the members of the Waldeck-Rousseau cabinet all favored Dreyfus's rehabilitation.[22]

In a dramatic reversal, the government had suddenly become Dreyfusard. However, despite the clear interest of the ministers in seeing Dreyfus go free, they could not control the military, and it was military judges who would once again decide the case. For the military to admit a mistake—or worse, a cover-up to hide a mistake—was almost unthinkable. As one officer at the time put it, "To declare Dreyfus innocent is one thing! But to condemn a general . . ."[23] Only an overpowering public demonstration of Dreyfus's innocence and Esterhazy's guilt would have the power to persuade the court.

To complicate matters further for the defense, major disagreements broke out between Demange and Labori, Dreyfus's two lawyers, who were opposed in terms of temperament and style. Demange wanted to avoid antagonizing the judges, while Labori thought the best path forward was to expose the full extent of the cover-up, even if this meant humiliating the military. The various larger-than-life personalities who had taken an interest in the case all attempted to weigh in on the best strategy. Clemenceau wanted to universalize the affair: by turning it into a crusade for truth and justice in general, and not just liberty for one man, he had helped widen the base of support for the Jewish officer. Others, such as Reinach, prioritized securing Dreyfus's freedom, even if this meant sacrificing loftier goals. Their disagreements created an atmosphere of tension, which even the diplomatic skills of Mathieu Dreyfus could not completely overcome.[24]

When Mathieu arrived in Rennes, the capital of Brittany, in the northwest of France, he found a city in a state of siege. Rennes had been chosen by the outgoing prime minister as the location for the new military court-martial because it was a reactionary stronghold, the capital of counter-revolutionary militancy and fundamentalist Catholic fervor. It was the least hospitable place for the Dreyfusards. Soldiers on both foot and horseback patrolled the streets, intending to maintain order.

Rennes had been taken over by trial participants, by spectators, and by the media—reporters from throughout France and the world had come to cover the most publicized trial of the nineteenth century. Mathieu and his wife went to see the prisoner on August 6, the day before the trial, and found the thirty-nine-year-old "very calm, full of serenity, extraordinarily confident." However, he looked frail. His hair had turned white and he spoke with difficulty—his voice had grown hoarse from disuse and several of his teeth had fallen out, causing a hissing sound when he talked.[25]

The trial took place at the lycée (high school) of Rennes, in a theater that had been transformed into a courtroom. Whereas the first court-martial had lasted three days, this one played out over five weeks, between August 7 and September 9, 1899. There was a deathly silence as Dreyfus entered the courtroom for the first time. The audience strained to catch a glimpse of the man who had become a symbol—for some of treachery, for others of victimhood. It was the first time he had been seen in public in five years, and his weakness was evident. "Never in my life will I forget the shock that seized me when Dreyfus was led into the hall," wrote Max Nordau, who was covering the trial for a Berlin newspaper. "What a tragedy!"[26] Mathieu instinctively shut his eyes when his brother entered. When he opened them, he saw his brother sitting erect before the judges, his pince-nez glasses perched on his thin face, his *képi*—the military hat with a flat circular top and visor—on his knees. Although Dreyfus had padded his uniform to disguise his skeletal frame, Mathieu could see that his brother's pants hung off his legs, which resembled long, thin sticks.[27]

As the presiding judge began interrogating his brother, Mathieu detected not a trace of sympathy in his manner. Dreyfus denied writing the bordereau yet again, but the crowd could barely hear his thin and raspy voice. The interrogators proceeded to rehash all the old accusations against him, concerning his supposed extramarital affairs and gambling debts. Dreyfus had never been able to charm, but he produced an especially robotic impression at Rennes. To Barrès, who saw Dreyfus up close for the first time, the Jewish soldier's reserve seemed monstrous: "He is lacking in a certain number of emotions without which we cannot conceive humanity."[28] Even some friendly spectators such as the diplomat Maurice Paléologue, who had taken an interest in the case after realizing that Henry had fabricated evidence, began to feel an instinctive mistrust at Dreyfus's almost mechanical responses to the hostile questions. "Why is this man incapable of putting any warmth into his words?" Paléologue wondered. "Why in his most vigorous protestations can nothing of his soul emerge through his strangled throat?"[29] Dreyfus's modesty prevented him from making a show of his emotions; his sincerity prevented him from exaggerating for effect. He continued to believe that such displays had nothing to do with what really mattered, which was his innocence, but he failed to understand that in the modern media world, when reporters scrutinized his every gesture, it was the appearance of innocence that mattered as much as if not more than the reality. His beleaguered demeanor, instead of eliciting sympathy, mostly inspired mistrust.

When it came time to review the infamous "secret file," the court decided to meet in closed session, citing national security concerns. This was a setback for the defense, since it once again meant that these supposedly damning documents would not be exposed to public scrutiny. On August 8, Mathieu wrote to Joseph Reinach, who had remained in Paris, that he "feared the worst." Moreover, rumors began to circulate that General Mercier would deliver a "staggering blow" to the defense in his testimony.[30]

When Mercier took the stand a few days later, he spoke for four hours, never once looking at the accused. He proceeded to explain the circumstances surrounding Dreyfus's arrest and first trial, when the army feared that revealing its evidence would provoke a war with Germany. Mercier then alluded to an incriminating document in which the German emperor had supposedly named Dreyfus as a spy, something that was all but inconceivable for a monarch to do. "At the castle in Potsdam everyone knew the name Dreyfus," the general nevertheless assured the court, without supplying the document in question. "If the slightest doubt had crossed my mind, gentlemen, I would be the first to tell you so," Mercier declared, "for I am an honest man and the son of an honest man. I would come before you to say to Captain Dreyfus: I erred in good faith."

At this point, Dreyfus rose and shouted: "That is what you should do!" When Mercier tried to continue his speech, Dreyfus again shouted: "It is your duty!" His outrage had finally been too great to repress. Applause erupted as Dreyfus's supporters thrilled to see the victim finally proclaim his innocence with passion. A visibly shaken Mercier hastily concluded his speech by maintaining that his belief in Dreyfus's guilt had not wavered since 1894. The Dreyfusards began to feel that things were going their way: aside from the allusion to an obviously apocryphal document, Mercier's testimony had added nothing concrete to the prosecution's case.

Their confidence was short-lived. Early in the morning of August 14, a Monday, Fernand Labori was headed to court alongside Colonel Picquart when they realized they were being followed. Suddenly a shot rang out and the lawyer fell to the ground, as the assailant escaped along the riverbank. Although he had been shot in the back, Labori miraculously sustained no lasting injuries. Telegrams of support arrived from across France and around the world. Zola, who had also stayed in Paris during the trial, wrote on August 16: "My dear, my great, my valiant friend, get better and complete our victory."[31] Dreyfus requested an adjournment of the proceedings until Labori recovered, but the court refused. Fortunately, the lawyer's convalescence was short, and he returned to the courtroom on August 22. Dreyfus's supporters expressed relief as Demange, Dreyfus's other advocate, lacked Labori's panache.[32]

By the time it came to the closing arguments, however, some felt that Labori had alienated the military judges by calling into question the integrity of the generals. Rumors circulated that Dreyfus would be exonerated if Labori did not take the floor at the conclusion of the trial. Mathieu was torn and shared his hesitations with both lawyers. In the end, Labori let Demange make the closing argument, not wanting to bear the responsibility if he spoke and Dreyfus was convicted. Demange's concluding oration lasted five hours on September 9, 1899. It was conciliatory, letting the military off the hook for the cover-up and conspiracy, focusing instead on technical matters pertaining to the case. Demange did not raise the question of anti-semitism. Labori found his tepid assertion of Dreyfus's innocence and ingratiating posture toward the judges pathetic, but he kept silent.[33]

As the judges withdrew to deliberate, the audience speculated on the verdict. Some thought the presiding judge's hostility was really a cover for his sympathy. Others read every harsh word and frown as a sign of Dreyfus's doom. "I am preparing myself methodically for the worst," wrote Nordau.[34] After only an hour and a half, bells rang to signal that a decision had been reached. The accused was not present as the judges delivered the verdict. By a vote of five votes to two, they found Dreyfus guilty, but with "extenuating circumstances." How there could be "extenuating circumstances" when it came to treason, the judges did not say, but it was a clear sign that the defense had instilled some doubt in the judges' minds even if they had not succeeded in convincing a majority to acquit. The sentence was ten years of detention. Dreyfus controlled his emotions, standing rigidly as a dejected Labori told him he would once more be stripped of his rank. "Take care of my wife and children," he said stoically before being led back to prison.

The nationalist and antisemitic press exulted. "The Traitor Condemned! Long Live the Army! Long Live France! Down with the Jews!" ran the headlines of the evening edition of *La Libre parole*.[35] Other voices on the right were more discreet yet no less jubilant. Although he denounced the presiding judge, who had in fact voted to acquit, Barrès praised the verdict: "The national conscience of France has been irritated and ruffled because foreigners both inside and outside of France wanted to 'put one over on us.' We acknowledge with immense hopefulness the victory at Rennes."[36]

The Dreyfusard press expressed outrage if not shock. "The Verdict of Cowardice," proclaimed the headline in *Le Siècle*, while Clemenceau in *L'Aurore*, under the optimistic headline "Toward Victory!" vowed to carry on the fight. Clemenceau predicted that the rest of the world would condemn France for its grotesque miscarriage of justice.[37]

The verdict indeed provoked outrage outside of France. As Hannah Arendt would later point out, the injustice inflicted on a single Jew during the affair produced a far greater and more unified international outcry than the persecution inflicted on millions of Jews during the Holocaust forty years later.[38] Even Tsarist Russia accused France of barbarism. As news of the verdict spread, anti-French demonstrations took place in Antwerp, Milan, Naples, and New York. In London on the night of Saturday, September 9, anti-French sentiment erupted in clubs and pubs, as well as in concert halls and theaters, where French performers were booed off the stage. The next day, London preachers condemned France in their sermons. At Westminster Abbey, Canon Robinson Duckworth thanked God that "we are citizens of a country whose tribunals are above suspicion." Over the following weeks, British newspapers received thousands of letters denouncing the injustice of the Rennes verdict. The *Daily News* proclaimed that it was "no longer Dreyfus, but France herself who is on trial," while the *Westminster Gazette* opined that "nothing in recent times has come as such a shock to civilization."[39]

American newspapers expressed shock and dismay at the verdict. This was the age of "yellow journalism," when newspapers competed to offer the most sensationalized reporting, and the coverage of the Dreyfus Affair was no exception. American journalists covered every dramatic development in the case, and they were overwhelmingly in the Dreyfusard camp. According to the *Atlanta Constitution*, if any American newspaper "insisted on the guilt of Dreyfus, or even hinted of its possibility, such demonstrations are not on record."[40] The various trials associated with the affair offered American journalists an opportunity to assert the superiority of American jurisprudence by criticizing the sloppy way in which French courts admitted evidence and examined witnesses. The case also offered American Protestants an opportunity to decry the role of the Catholic Church in French politics.

Even more than in other parts of the world, support for Dreyfus in the United States was accompanied by outspoken opposition to antisemitism. In *Harper's Weekly*, Carl Schurz explained that Dreyfus had been scapegoated for being a Jew, and went on to denounce antisemitism as "that meanest and most hideous remnant of medieval barbarism."[41] Shortly before the Rennes trial, Mark Twain praised Zola for his role in the case and called Dreyfus "the most infamously misused Jew of modern times."[42] After the Rennes trial, the *New York Times* warned, "The verdict, they say, is directed more against the Jews than against Dreyfus, and, if allowed to stand, will make their existence in France impossible."[43] Such sensitivity to discrimination may seem surprising, given the high level of nativist resentment in the United States at the time, but the Dreyfus Affair allowed

Museum of Horrors, No. 35: Popular Amnesty! (Imp. Lenepveu, 1900)

Americans like Schurz and Twain to recognize the danger that antisemitism posed for liberal democracy in France and gave them the opportunity to warn against those dangers at home.[44]

That America at the turn of the twentieth century was hardly a model of racial justice did not escape the notice of certain observers, who used the Dreyfus Affair to call attention to anti-Black racism in the United States. Albion Tourgée, the American consul in Bordeaux, sent dispatches about the Dreyfus case to President William McKinley, comparing French antisemitism to lynching in the American South. The anti-lynching activist Ida B. Wells-Barnett described how "the conscience of this country was shocked" at the Rennes verdict, but went on to point out that despite an understandable sympathy for Dreyfus, "in our own land and under our own flag, the writer can give day and detail of one thousand men, women, and children who during the last six years were put to death without trial before any tribunal on earth."[45] And in his *Autobiography*, W. E. B. Du Bois describes how he followed the Dreyfus case and gained sympathy for the "plight of other minority groups" because of the history of Black lynching in the United States.[46] Tourgée, Wells-Barnett, and Du Bois were not the only ones to draw a parallel between Dreyfus and Black victims in the American South: one of the three Museum of Horrors posters depicting Dreyfus shows him hanging by the neck, a probable reference to the American practice of lynching, since most French public executions at the time were by guillotine. It reveals the extent to which the European antisemitic imagination was fed by anti-Black racism in the United States.

Although the danger posed to French citizens and embassies abroad quickly dissipated, French authorities worried about growing calls to boycott the upcoming Paris World's Fair of 1900 in protest against the Rennes verdict. French prestige, and a massive financial investment in the fair, were on the line. The threat of civil disturbance also spurred Waldeck-Rousseau to search for ways to resolve the case. Reinach suggested that the French government should take immediate action by offering Dreyfus a pardon. The republic overruling the military courts and declaring Dreyfus innocent would send a strong signal to right-wing groups at home, Reinach argued. By freeing "France from any complicity with injustice," it would silence critics abroad. A pardon was not the equivalent of a complete rehabilitation for Dreyfus, but it could serve as a transitional measure. And it would mean that the physically weakened Dreyfus would not have to return to prison.[47]

But would the Dreyfusards agree to a pardon if it meant withdrawing their petition for a revision of the Rennes verdict? Clemenceau, who always emphasized that the affair was not about one man's freedom but about the universal principle of justice free from military or government intervention, opposed the idea: "You are humiliating the Republic before the saber," he declared at a meeting of the leading Dreyfusards. Jaurès, the Socialist leader, at first agreed with Clemenceau, but he also understood that Dreyfus's life was on the line. He accepted the idea of the pardon provided that Dreyfus could continue to fight for complete exoneration at a later date.[48]

Armed with promises from the government ministers, Mathieu went to see his brother in the Rennes prison. At first Dreyfus rejected the idea of the pardon: "I only craved justice," he wrote in his *Souvenirs*. But eventually Mathieu was able to convince him that a pardon would serve as a rebuke to the military court. Mathieu also reminded his brother that a pardon would return him to his wife and children. On September 19, 1899, President Émile Loubet signed the decree making Dreyfus a free man. The next day, newspapers printed Dreyfus's statement, "The government of the Republic restores me to liberty. It means nothing to me without honor. Starting today, I will continue to pursue reparation for the horrifying judicial error of which I am still a victim."[49]

Dreyfus left the prison in Rennes in the middle of the night, surrounded by five security agents. Mathieu carried a revolver as they boarded a train headed for the South, to their sister Henriette Valabrègue's home in Carpentras. Despite the precautions, and the fight for justice that lay ahead, Dreyfus felt the joy of being a free man as the French countryside unfurled through the train windows. "I felt like I had been reborn after a long and horrible nightmare," he wrote.[50]

Henriette had always served as a kind of second mother to Dreyfus, and her estate offered protection from the prying eyes of journalists. It was in Carpentras that Dreyfus finally reunited with Lucie and the children, Pierre and Jeanne. At first, he feared that his children wouldn't recognize the father they hadn't seen for almost five years, who had grown so frail that he barely resembled his former self. But Lucie had kept his memory alive during his absence, and the children threw themselves into his arms. "The following days offered moments of tender intimacy," Dreyfus wrote. "And also of rest, which we all needed so badly."[51]

Over the next few weeks, Dreyfus met with some of the supporters who had devoted themselves to his cause. Many came away disappointed. Reinach describes how Dreyfus failed to live up to the heroic image of the victim that the Dreyfusards had cherished. "They generally found that Dreyfus continued to play his role badly, when in reality he was not playing any role at all." What the frustrated supporters failed to realize, according to Reinach, who made the trip to Carpentras in October 1899, was that Dreyfus's understated demeanor was not a sign of coldness or ingratitude, but rather of modesty and dignity in the face of suffering. "His obstinate pride prevented him from appealing to pity," Reinach wrote. He even chafed at the attention of his wife and sister, when they expressed too much concern for his physical condition.[52]

The Dreyfusard coalition quickly unraveled after the prisoner's release. Although most of his supporters had accepted, or at least understood, the necessity of the pardon, many strongly opposed the plan for a general amnesty that the government floated that fall. Clemenceau expressed outrage that the orchestrators of the cover-up in the military would escape punishment for their crime: "They are accomplices. Now they demand amnesty. Amnesty for them, to be sure. The innocent man will rest content with his dishonored pardon."[53] Labori and Picquart sided with Clemenceau, as did Jaurès and Zola. They expressed contempt for Reinach and the Dreyfuses, who they thought had cut a deal with Waldeck-Rousseau to sweep the whole affair under the rug. Picquart was especially outraged that his own amnesty would be paired with that of the generals who had acted so dishonorably, such as Mercier.

The pardon of Dreyfus produced relatively little protest from right-wing groups. So did Déroulède's trial that fall. However, Waldeck-Rousseau still feared unrest, and pushed through a general amnesty that swept away all lawsuits and criminal acts relative to the case with the sole exception of the Rennes verdict so that Dreyfus could pursue his appeal. Zola objected, as did Dreyfus himself, who demanded that miscreants like Mercier be brought to justice. With the World's Fair a success, and the passions surrounding the affair subsiding for all but those most implicated in it, the legislature passed the amnesty law in December 1900.

If anyone can be said to have emerged a winner from the Dreyfus Affair, it was Waldeck-Rousseau. The government of republican defense triumphed in the elections of 1901. Then, either worn out by all the struggle or not willing to govern his increasingly emboldened leftist coalition, Waldeck-Rousseau abruptly announced that he was stepping down. With the right wing in disarray, the government of Émile Combes, who succeeded Waldeck-Rousseau as prime minister in June 1902, proceeded to consolidate the gains of the Dreyfusard left. The main goal of the new government was the complete separation of church and state, which the left saw as necessary to prevent the Catholic clergy from exercising the kind of reactionary influence they had during the affair. The so-called Combes law, which separated church and state, enshrining the notion of French secularism or *laïcité* that we know today, passed on December 9, 1905. It was one of the most long-lasting effects of the affair in France.

After his pardon, Dreyfus received letters of congratulations along with many invitations. Lady Stanley, the wife of the African explorer Henry Morton Stanley, offered up her country home in England. A friend of the Dreyfus family offered a villa in Cannes. The citizens of Otsego, Michigan—a town of about two thousand people on the banks of the Kalamazoo River, known for its paper mills—proposed purchasing a house for Dreyfus, as did a well-wisher from Louisville, Kentucky, in the hope that he would settle permanently in the United States, an honor he graciously refused.[54]

Eventually, the Dreyfuses decided to accept the offer of their friends, the Swiss Protestant Naville family, to visit them at their villa outside Geneva. Switzerland was familiar to Alfred from his childhood sojourn in Basel, and its clear mountain air provided the perfect retreat for him to recuperate from the physical and emotional strain he had endured on Devil's Island and during his trial at Rennes. He spent his days gazing at the beautiful scenery and receiving visits from well-wishers. "What an exquisite rest this was for all of us after so many painful years," he wrote.[55]

Although Alfred continued to suffer from ailments brought about by his ordeal, the Dreyfuses returned to Paris in the fall of 1900, stung by false accusations that they had accepted exile in return for the pardon. Some of his close supporters, including Reinach and Zola, understood his need for rest, but others such as Clemenceau, Picquart, and Labori resented that Dreyfus was relaxing in Switzerland while they continued to fight the forces of reaction back in Paris. They stopped speaking to Mathieu, who soon returned to Mulhouse to rejoin the family business. Caught between devotion to his brother and gratitude toward his former supporters, Dreyfus found these quarrels "painful" and "nerve-racking." The efforts to mediate between the two camps brought on a return of malarial fever.[56]

Dreyfus arrived back in Paris just as the World's Fair was winding down. It had been a great success, showcasing a number of recent inventions, including the Ferris wheel, the moving sidewalk, and the Palace of Electricity, a gigantic building capped by a torch powered by 50,000 volts of electric power. Paris was trying its best to put the controversy of the affair behind it and recover its reputation as the City of Light.

For Dreyfus and his supporters, however, the affair would not end until they had achieved justice, which is to say complete exoneration. This remained an uphill battle. To request a revision of the Rennes verdict, they needed to bring to light new evidence that the judges had not considered. Hoping to turn up something they could use, Jaurès managed to persuade the Chamber of Deputies to examine all the documents in the secret dossier yet again. The investigation, which lasted six months, revealed several forgeries by Henry that had not been accounted for at the Rennes trial. This was enough to allow Dreyfus to make his petition. "I request the revision of my trial," he wrote in 1903, "because I require all of my honor, for my children and myself, because I have never been remiss in any of my duties as a soldier and a Frenchman."[57] On December 24, 1903, the Council of Ministers decided that Dreyfus had grounds for a revision and referred the matter to the High Court of Appeal, which also had jurisdiction over military courts. There would be yet another trial. It would take until the summer of 1906 for the High Court of Appeal to hear the case. This time, Dreyfus and supporters were confident that it would be the last.

From the beginning, this trial looked nothing like the previous ones, which had been designed to prevent the truth from coming to light. This time, the court displayed a clear sympathy toward Dreyfus. In his presentation to the court, the public

prosecutor Manuel Baudoin emphasized the grotesque violation of justice that Dreyfus had experienced at the hands of
military. Significantly, he did not shy away from attributing the
military's actions, from the initial accusation to the later cover-
up, to antisemitic prejudice. It was one of the rare instances during the affair in which a government spokesman acknowledged
that anti-Jewish attitudes had been an issue in the case.[58]

In his own presentation, Dreyfus's new lawyer, Henri Mornard, largely echoed Baudoin, but went even further in denouncing the role played by antisemitism: "All the irregularities of the
investigation, all the felonies, all the crimes committed against
the accused were only the logical result of the antisemitic rea-
soning built on the basis of one fundamental belief: the necessary treachery of the Jew. . . . It is this antisemitic belief system
which dominated the brains of all those improvised magistrates
. . . and annihilated in them all their faculties of reason." According to Mornard, in any ordinary case, when evidence was
found lacking, the case would be dropped. But not for Dreyfus:
"When the basis of the accusation collapsed, the Jew remained
no less a traitor in his essence. The system of the accusation was
secondary, a sort of envelope or cloak to cover an untouchable
dogma: the treachery of Judas."[59] Mornard went on to elaborate
on the ways in which the leading players in the conspiracy against
Dreyfus—Sandherr, Mercier, and the rest—were motivated, first
and foremost, by antisemitic hatred.

As Duclert points out, Mornard would not have been able
to place such importance on the question of antisemitism at the
final trial without the consent of Dreyfus himself.[60] Although
the Jewish officer was too discreet to broach the question in any
of his published writing about the affair, the fact that he allowed
his lawyer to make antisemitism the cornerstone of his theory of
the case shows the great importance he attributed to it. Rarely,
until very recently, has antisemitism received a more forceful
public denunciation in France. For Mornard, and by extension

for Dreyfus, antisemitism was a crime against Jews, but it was also a crime against democracy. Mornard made clear that the health of the republic depended on eradicating such prejudice from its institutions: "It is demoralizing for the public spirit to let racial and religious hatred continue into the twentieth century to stop the course of justice, to introduce errors and to indefinitely prohibit their repair."[61]

This time, the judges agreed. Unencumbered by the pressures that had weighed on the military court, which could not bring itself to expose so many top generals as liars, the High Court of Appeal was free to follow the evidence. On July 12, 1906, the court handed down the final verdict, completely exonerating Dreyfus of the crime of treason. "Nothing whatever remains of the charges brought against Dreyfus," the judges declared. "The supreme jurisdiction of the country has repaired the monstrous judicial error of the military judges," affirmed *Le Siècle*.[62] *L'Aurore* devoted its entire first page to the news under a banner headline proclaiming simply: "Justice."[63] As part of the process of rehabilitation, on July 13, the Chamber of Deputies voted to reintegrate Dreyfus into the army at the rank of major (*chef d'escadron*).

Letters and telegrams of congratulations flooded in from around the world. By July 24, the Dreyfus family had received more than ten thousand such messages.[64] However, the official reaction of the French Jewish community was muted. Choosing to interpret the victory as a vindication of their faith in French institutions and in the French universalist tradition, Jewish organizations decided that it was inappropriate to call attention as Jews to the happy outcome of the affair. When one of the members of the Central Consistory, the governing body of French Judaism, suggested sending a letter of congratulations to the Dreyfus family, the idea was rejected.[65]

On July 21, 1906, troops assembled in a small courtyard of the École militaire, near where Dreyfus's degradation had taken place twelve years before. At 1:30 P.M., Major Dreyfus, wearing full military dress, entered the arena. At 1:55 trumpets sounded. Dreyfus stepped forward, stiff and upright as he had been when his insignia were stripped from his uniform and his sword broken in two. Memories of that horrible day in 1894 flashed through his mind. His heart began to beat fast and sweat covered his brow. "It took enormous will power," he wrote, "to regain control and not allow my former sorrows to burst forth." This time, however, a general tapped him with a sword on the shoulder three times and proclaimed, "In the name of the president of the Republic, and by virtue of the powers invested in me, I hereby name you Knight of the Legion of Honor." As Dreyfus finally received the congratulations of his fellow officers that he had sought in vain when he returned from Devil's Island, he heard cries of "Long live Dreyfus!" from the troops.

"No," he responded solemnly. "Long live the Republic! Long live the truth!"[66]

6

The Reaction

"I DOUBT IF the Dreyfus case made such a stir anywhere as it did in Kasrilevke," claims the narrator in Sholem Aleichem's comic short story about the inhabitants of a fictional Ukrainian shtetl who become overly invested in the affair. Published in a Yiddish newspaper in 1902, "Dreyfus in Kasrilevke" describes how the small-town Jews learn about the affair from the rabbi's son Zeidel, the only one among them to subscribe to a newspaper. So great is their interest in the case that the townspeople begin to follow Zeidel to his house to get the latest news about Dreyfus more quickly and then to the post office to intercept him as soon as he receives his paper.[1]

Sholem Aleichem's story offers an indication of the powerful effect the Dreyfus Affair had on Jewish communities around the world. Of course, non-Jews took an interest in the case as well, but for Jews the affair was an obsession. From London to Sydney, from St. Petersburg to Cincinnati, Jewish readers devoured dispatches from Devil's Island, interviews with Lucie, and accounts of Dreyfus's legal maneuvers in Jewish newspapers that often seemed to report on little else. Nor was news of the affair confined to the printed word. We have already encountered the pervasive antisemitic imagery of the affair, but an equal quantity of visual material sympathetic to Dreyfus—illustrated books, posters, and even board games—captured the world's attention. Postcards, featuring the likenesses of the main actors or illustrations from the courtroom, were particularly well-suited to international circulation.

The affair coincided with the rise of a new form of mass culture, which found in the case the perfect subject to hook consumers, especially Jewish ones. As Susan Rubin Suleiman has shown, pulp fiction in multiple languages turned the affair into both a swashbuckling adventure and a sentimental love story.[2] Plays about the affair directed at immigrant audiences packed theaters in New York and Chicago. "Who has not read about the sad case of Captain Dreyfus? What Jew is not concerned with his plight?" asked the poster for a play by the Yiddish dramatist Jacob Gordin starring Jacob P. Adler. Mothers in Bukovina sang the Yiddish lullaby "Drayfusl mayn kind," while American teenagers could dance to the "Dreyfus March Two-Step."[3] And religious publishers jumped on the bandwagon as well: observant Jews could celebrate Purim with an illustrated Megillah based on the case: the story of the Jews' triumph over their enemies told in Yiddish, English, and French, with Esterhazy and Henry substituted for the role of the evil Haman.[4]

However, if the affair lent itself to light entertainment for the Jewish masses, it also spurred serious debates about the Jewish future. These debates had raged for years but became especially fierce with the creation in 1897 of the Zionist movement, which advocated for Jews to form their own nation in Palestine. As the affair came to a head in the years that followed, the

Zionists faced strong opposition from the Jewish establishment. Before the Holocaust and the foundation of the state of Israel encouraged widespread support for Zionism, most middle-class Jews practiced a form of what David Sorkin calls "emancipation politics," fighting for Jews to gain equal rights and advocating for Jews to become loyal citizens of the countries in which they were born. As the nineteenth century drew to a close, both these establishment Jews, whom I will label "integrationists," and the Zionists were opposed by the Socialists, who rejected all forms of nationalism in favor of working-class solidarity. Many orthodox and ultra-orthodox Jews, meanwhile, looked askance at all these forms of Jewish politics, but tended to ally with the integrationists. In this chapter, I widen my focus beyond Dreyfus himself to explore how his life played a defining role for these three competing Jewish political ideologies at a crucial moment in their development.[5]

Indeed, these debates turn out to be the real subject of Sholem Aleichem's story. The Jews of Kasrilevke, accustomed to oppression at home but not in the West, believe in the French justice system and place their faith in gentile heroes such as Picquart, Zola, and Labori. Implicit integrationists, they are shocked when the Rennes verdict declares Dreyfus guilty a second time and take out their frustrations on Zeidel, the bearer of the bad news. "How could such an ugly thing happen in Paris?" they demand to know, refusing to abandon their trust in the French model of emancipation. Zeidel, a realist, harbors no such illusions: "'Fools!' shouted Zeidel, and thrust the paper into their faces. 'Look! See what the paper says!'" In his rejection of the townspeople's faith in France and its ideals, Zeidel might be said to incarnate the Zionist position, which encouraged Jews to "emancipate themselves" by seeking national autonomy. Although Sholem Aleichem himself was a supporter of Zionism, the story's final sentence—"And—who was right?"—shows to what extent the "Jewish Question" remained an open one at the time, especially for Jews.

ZIONISTS

According to Hannah Arendt, the most significant result of the Dreyfus Affair, as far as Jews were concerned, was that "it gave birth to the Zionist movement."[6] The assumption that the affair led to Zionism can be traced directly to Theodor Herzl himself, the founder of the modern Zionist movement, who claimed in an essay in 1899 that "what made me a Zionist was the Dreyfus trial." Herzl described hearing the crowd at the École militaire chanting "Death to the Jews!" as he covered Dreyfus's degradation for Vienna's *Neue Freie Presse* and thinking that if such antisemitism could break out even in enlightened France, then Jews would only be safe once they had a homeland of their own.[7]

Scholars now recognize that Herzl's version of events was more myth than reality: his coverage of the degradation ceremony did not mention antisemitism and he most likely assumed—as did everyone else—that Dreyfus was guilty. It seems that Herzl believed he would enhance the image of Zionism if he could claim to have foreseen as early as 1895 the way the antisemitism unleashed by the affair would shake the foundations of the French republic. And yet, even if the Dreyfus Affair did not lie at the origin of Zionism, without question it played a transformational role in the development of the Zionist movement.[8]

Die Welt, the Vienna-based Zionist newspaper founded by Herzl in May 1897, used its in-depth coverage of the affair to build support for the Zionist project. *Die Welt* relentlessly faulted both the leadership of the French Jewish community for failing to rush to defend Dreyfus and France as a whole for its betrayal of the Jews: "No voice for justice is to be found in the entire country," asserted one *Die Welt* report in November 1897. "In this very land it appears that forty million people are willing accomplices to barbarism and declare with glee and scorn that 'for Jews there is no justice!'"⁹ An article on debates in the French Chamber of Deputies summarized *Die Welt*'s understanding of the affair:

> We Zionists again learned something out of this parliamentary session. We Jews have nothing to expect from this "civilized" Europe. Antisemitism progressed more than the worst pessimist amongst us could have guessed. The so-called moderate parties are steeped in antisemitism. In their eyes, too, we are foreigners, nothing but foreigners. Our homeland [*Heimat*] is somewhere else. Our real mother country [*Vaterland*] still awaits.
>
> Besides many other events, this parliamentary session will also have taught French Jews that there is only one real salvation, one definitive solution—Zionism.¹⁰

For Herzl, the affair proved once and for all the bankruptcy of the French model of integration and demonstrated the necessity for Jews to exercise sovereignty in a state of their own.¹¹

Herzl's interpretation of the affair found an echo in other newspapers favorable to Jewish nationalism. Like *Die Welt*, the leading Hebrew-language journals in the Russian empire, despite heavy censorship, used their coverage of the affair to call attention to the crisis of antisemitism and to the failure of the French model of emancipation. The Warsaw-based *Ha-Tsefira* lamented repeatedly that Jews could not trust European state institutions. *Ha-Melits*, published in St. Petersburg, was quick to see the case against Dreyfus as an antisemitic conspiracy and to call attention to the anti-Jewish violence that resulted from the publication of Zola's "J'Accuse." *Ha-Melits* also heaped scorn on the emancipated Jewry of Western Europe, referring to "our brethren in France, asleep with the storm around them."¹²

The Zionist interpretation of the affair was reflected in a striking parable published in *Ha-Melits* on May 13, 1898. Entitled "In the Jordan Valley" and dedicated to the Jewish nationalist Leon Pinsker, the piece describes a mystical vision that the author Brazili supposedly had on a trip to Jerusalem, where he saw a trial taking place and heard the names Dreyfus and Esterhazy. A mysterious guide then led the author to a valley full of human bones, which had lain there for two thousand years, picked apart by wolves and unable to find peace. The author heard the skeletons demand to return to "the land of life," where they would once again be able to breathe the air and acquire flesh. Although the author does not interpret his vision, the message of the parable is clear: the valley of bones represents the Jews of the diaspora, condemned to constant suffering, who long to be restored to the Jewish homeland in Palestine, the "land of life." Dreyfus's trial thus serves as the catalyst for the Zionist dream.

As we have seen, the affair pushed Bernard Lazare to embrace the cause of Jewish nationalism. But as Robert S. Wistrich has noted, it was the Paris-based journalist Max Nordau who gave the most authoritative Zionist interpretation of the affair. Like Herzl, Nordau covered Dreyfus's degradation ceremony for a German-language newspaper and, like him, credited the antisemitism he witnessed there for his Zionist conversion. Adopting a prophetic tone, Nordau underscored in his address to the Second Zionist Congress of 1898 how the Dreyfus case had proved once and for all the failure of the French model of emancipation as a solution to the "Jewish Question":

> It [the Dreyfus Affair] addresses itself as a warning and a lesson to those Jews who still absolutely want to believe in their definitive, unreserved acceptance in the national community, at least of the most advanced States of the West. That is its significance in Jewish history and this even gives it the serious educational value of an admonition, a piece of enlightenment and a punishment—an importance which enables us with our inextinguishable Jewish optimism to proclaim even when faced with the Dreyfus case: "Gam zu le-tova!" [This, too, is for the best!"].[13]

Nordau covered the Rennes trial the following year in an almost feverish state of anxiety. The judgment against Dreyfus left him shattered, more convinced than ever that Jews must leave Europe for Palestine.[14]

Notably, most Zionist writers did not alter their understanding of the affair once Dreyfus gained his freedom. Although Nordau described France's government of republican defense that offered Dreyfus a pardon in positive terms, and later called Waldeck-Rousseau a "true statesman," he also feared that the anticlericalism of the Dreyfusard left would inspire a backlash against Jews.[15] The Zionist-leaning Hebrew press echoed Nordau's concerns. In a "Letter from France," published on August 15, 1904, a journalist for *Ha-Tsefira* argued that antisemitism remained pervasive in France, despite the positive outcome of the affair; in another, published on September 1, 1904, that the Dreyfus case made more Jews dream of a national homeland: "Jews have no problem at all to decide, even today, that we are one people as Herzl and Nordau explicitly said."

INTEGRATIONISTS

For those Jewish intellectuals on the other end of the ideological spectrum, who believed that Jews should integrate into the nations of their birth while still remaining Jews, the affair posed a dilemma. On one hand, integrated Jews saw the injustice perpetrated upon Dreyfus as a violation of the premise of emancipation, which offered Jews equality under the law. They felt deeply threatened by the antisemitism unleashed by the affair and wanted to combat it. On the other hand, they feared that overemphasizing the threat risked undermining confidence in the path of integration and thereby encouraging the Zionist movement. This conflict played out across the pages of the Jewish newspapers published in European languages (French, German, Polish, English, and others).

In France, the two leading Jewish newspapers had existed

since the early 1840s. Although different in terms of their approach to religious matters—*Les Archives israélites* was reformist in outlook, whereas *L'Univers israélite* was orthodox—they nevertheless shared a commitment to Jewish integration within the republican state and an opposition both to total assimilation and to Zionism.

The initial coverage of Dreyfus's arrest in both newspapers betrayed a deep anxiety: "Our interests are threatened, our rights are neglected, the security of our future is insufficiently protected," warned the editor of *Les Archives israélites* after Dreyfus's conviction.[16] Once it began to become clear that Dreyfus was innocent, however, the papers adopted a more combative posture, not fearing to denounce the dark forces allied against the Jewish officer. "It is antisemitism which, by bringing into the work of justice considerations of race and religion, has seriously undermined the cause of justice," declared *L'Univers israélite* in 1896.[17]

As the affair dragged on, both papers reaffirmed their faith in the French republic. However, they did so with a new understanding of what they required in exchange for their loyalty. "The Republic, if it is not to betray its mission, cannot tolerate any attack on the principles of public tranquility and social fraternity which are contested, disputed, and abused in the form of antisemitism by the reactionaries and the clericals," declared *Les Archives israélites* in March 1898, as the antisemitic riots raged throughout France. "Absolute and perfect equality, that is what French Israelites expect of the Republic."[18] On the eve of the Rennes trial, an article in *L'Univers israélite* concluded that the affair had actually been good for French Jews because it taught them to fight for their rights: "We were too inclined to be lulled into a false security," the author said of Jewish life in France before the affair. "In revealing to us the danger, [the affair] forced us to combat it."[19]

Although the two French Jewish newspapers rarely diverged

in their coverage of the affair, conflict erupted over whether Dreyfus should continue his fight once he had been pardoned. After *Les Archives israélites* suggested that it might be better to avoid reopening the case for fear of reawakening antisemitism, an editorial in *L'Univers israélite* denounced the cowardice of its reformist rival. Eventually the *Archives* came around. By the time of Dreyfus's exoneration in 1906, both newspapers were quick to point to the lack of reaction by the antisemites as proof that the republic had weathered the crisis of the affair and that Jews were once again safe in France.

Integrationist Jewish newspapers in other countries used their coverage of the affair to underscore how the situation in their respective nations was much less dangerous for Jews than in France. The leading exponent of integrationist ideology in Germany, the *Allgemeine Zeitung des Judentums*, was founded in 1837, slightly before the French Jewish newspapers that modeled themselves on it. In its articles reporting on the case, the German newspaper registered alarm at the rise of antisemitism in France while simultaneously—and ironically, given subsequent historical developments—dismissing its consequences for German Jews. In their coverage of the affair, the writers for the *Allgemeine Zeitung* mainly blamed the outbreak of antisemitism on the French political system, when they did not overtly blame it on the Zionists, as in an article titled "The End of Zionism," from February 1899, which accused the Jewish nationalists of arousing anti-Jewish hatred by displaying disloyalty to the nations of their birth.[20]

Along with extensive coverage of Dreyfus's legal battle, the *Allgemeine Zeitung* published two reflective essays about the affair by the German Jewish philosopher Hermann Cohen. One of the few Jews to hold a professorship at a German university, Cohen was a critic of Zionism who saw the affair as a test of his integrationist beliefs. The first, "Our Obligation of Honor Toward Dreyfus," published just prior to the Rennes trial, characterized Dreyfus as "a martyr of our faith," whose "biography hence-forth forms an important page in the more recent history of the Jews." Cohen expressed the hope that a not-guilty verdict at Rennes would "redeem" the Jews from accusations of immorality and would prevent more German Jews from abandoning their religion as a result.[21] Although disappointed in 1899, Cohen found satisfaction in 1906, with Dreyfus's eventual exoneration. His later piece, "The Historical Significance of the Conclusion of the Dreyfus Affair," argued that the triumph of justice in the Dreyfus case proved that Jews belong in Europe and that Zion-ism is little more than a "pious wish [*frommer Wunsch*]."[22]

In Congress Poland (then a part of the Russian empire), integrationist views found their fullest expression in the news-paper *Izraelita*. Articles in this Polish-language journal sought to defend Dreyfus and denounce antisemitism, while simulta-neously affirming that Jews still had a place in the French re-public. They remained largely optimistic throughout the affair that "step by step, truth will in the end triumph."[23] In 1906, a time when Jews in Poland faced renewed discrimination, *Izra-elita* exulted that "the Dreyfus Affair and its solution have de-stroyed antisemitism in France."[24] But this persistent optimism did not convince all readers. According to Antony Polonsky, the effect of the affair on Eastern European Jewish intellectuals was to shift the balance of power away from the integrationists and toward the Jewish nationalists.[25]

The leading integrationist British Jewish newspaper, the *Jewish Chronicle*, founded in 1841, took a strong stand in defense of Dreyfus from the start, denying that a Jew would ever betray his country.[26] As the affair heated up, the *Jewish Chronicle* began devoting a section to the case in every issue of the paper, cover-ing both Dreyfus's quest for justice and the antisemitism that it unleashed, often alongside disparaging reports about the attrac-tion of immigrant Jews to the Zionist movement, which they saw as dangerous and disloyal. The events in France allowed the

Chronicle's editors to appreciate the factors that made them safer than their French co-religionists. Asserting the superiority of British national traditions, especially the British legal system, the *Chronicle* tended to attribute the unrest across the Channel either to French "decadence" or to France's long-standing tendency toward mob violence. They nevertheless expressed hope that the French would eventually come to their senses.[27]

The editors of the *Jewish Chronicle*, like the characters in Sholem Aleichem's story and Jews across the world, were shocked by the verdict at the Rennes trial, which they called both a "gross injustice" and "the triumph of hate."[28] The *Chronicle* saw the verdict as a test not just for Dreyfus but for all Jews, who "must await with calm confidence the vindication of their sorely-tried brother in faith."[29] When the pardon and eventual exoneration justified their patient approach, the *Chronicle* rejoiced at the spectacle of "a great Western country deliberately shaking itself free from the strangulating influence of anti-Semitism." The *Jewish Chronicle* would soon come to embrace Zionism, but for the time being, it viewed the happy outcome of the affair as confirmation that integration remained the correct answer to the "Jewish Question."[30]

The first of hundreds of articles to report on the Dreyfus Affair in the *American Israelite*, the organ of reformed Judaism founded in Cincinnati in 1854, assumed the guilt of the Jewish officer, comparing him to the American traitor Benedict Arnold and expressing sorrow that the abolition of capital punishment in France meant that he could not be put to death. Describing the "blush of shame" that his arrest brought to cheeks of Jews around the world, the author argued that "just as no race or religion brings an exclusive assurance of honorable living, so none can be held to blame when one of its members or adherents falls far below the standard they have set up."[31] Another piece reported that a Jewish debutante in St. Louis named Emma Dreyfus, "by the advice of influential friends," changed her name before coming out.[32] Once the newspaper received reports of Dreyfus's innocence, however, its approach shifted. Like the *Jewish Chronicle* in London, it now declared the necessity to vindicate the Jewish officer for the sake of "all Israel, which has not escaped calumny."[33]

Like their counterparts in Europe, integrated American Jews struggled to reconcile the antisemitism of the Dreyfus Affair with their faith that Jews could achieve equality inside the framework of liberal democracy. The Dreyfus Affair took place at a time of enormous change for the American Jewish community, as millions of newly arrived Eastern European Jews crowded into the nation's cities, especially on the East Coast. The largely German Jewish writers and readers of the *American Israelite*, already middle class and midwestern for several generations, looked on these poor, orthodox Yiddish speakers with a measure of disdain and alarm, fearing that their enormous numbers, cultural differences, and radical political tendencies would awaken antisemitism in the United States. Covered alongside the growth of the Zionist movement, the antisemitism unleashed by the Dreyfus Affair was viewed through the same lens, both developments seen as dangers to overcome.

As early as 1895, the newspaper raised the possibility that the Jewish captain had fallen victim not just to a judicial error but to an antisemitic plot. One suspects that the editors of the *American Israelite* might have felt less sympathy had Dreyfus been a poor immigrant from Eastern Europe, but when they learned that he was from "one of the oldest, richest, and most influential" Jewish families in France, they began to denounce the prejudice at the root of the case.[34] The specter of antisemitism curtailing the rights of a wealthy, well-integrated Jew clearly struck fear into the hearts of the *American Israelite* writers and readers, calling into question the very premises of emancipation. "The world, and especially the republican world, has a right to know what justice, honor and patriotism signify in a military court in France," one editorial demanded.[35]

The *American Israelite* adopted a posture meant simultaneously to arouse the indignation of its acculturated readers at the dangers facing the Jews of France and to reassure them of their own safety on American shores. "The whole thing seems strange to an American," the editors wrote, thanking God that such a miscarriage of justice could not happen "in our country."[36] The belief in American exceptionalism guided the journal's detailed coverage of the disturbing rise of anti-Jewish sentiment in France. "The program of the French anti-Semites seems almost incredible to American citizens habituated to the tolerant spirit which is embodied in our Federal Constitution," began one article on the violence against Jews in Algeria that followed the publication of Zola's "J'Accuse."[37] Expressions of antisemitism in the United States—the exclusion of Jews from many clubs and hotels, as well as from certain elite schools and professions, including the officer corps of the army—were routinely minimized by the *American Israelite*.

French Jews in the nineteenth century enjoyed much greater levels of integration than Jews in the United States, and the editors of the *American Israelite* struggled to explain why antisemitism there had suddenly become so pronounced. Whereas the *Jewish Chronicle* argued that the French had become "decadent," the *American Israelite*'s explanation for the recent turn of events was that France had become "degenerate." (*Degeneration* was the title of a book by Max Nordau in 1892 denouncing the depravity of fin-de-siècle French culture.) In their impotent rage at falling behind other countries, the French masses turned against the Jews, the newspaper explained. The implication was that Jews in the United States, a country clearly on the ascent, had nothing to fear.[38]

The *American Israelite* was not alone in pointing to the inferiority of French institutions: much of its coverage recycled the analysis of the affair that was being published in mainstream (non-Jewish) English-language newspapers, both British and American, which highlighted three main areas in which France lagged in comparison to Anglo-American customs and norms. The first was the excessive French patriotism that took hold after the loss of Alsace and Lorraine in 1871. It was the French cult of militarism, critics alleged, that jeopardized the rights of the individual by elevating military law over civil law. The second was the French justice system itself, which left English and American reporters at the Rennes trial aghast at the way evidence was handled and the lack of cross-examination of witnesses. The final source of French inferiority, and the most fundamental, in their eyes, was the influence of the Catholic Church, and especially the Jesuits, in French governmental affairs. The writers for the *American Israelite* showed no qualms about adopting the anti-Catholic prejudices of the mainstream Anglo-American press to explain why Jews were so much safer in Protestant-dominated England and America.[39]

As in other integrationist newspapers, the Zionist thesis that Jews should leave the diaspora in response to antisemitism met with scorn on the pages of the *American Israelite*. In the April 7, 1899, edition, for example, articles referred to Zionism as both a "folly" and an "absurdity." Reporting on a recent meeting of Zionists in Syracuse, New York, "at which those [who] attended were mainly, almost exclusively, recent immigrants from Eastern Europe," the paper mocked one speaker for advocating the formation of a Jewish state in Palestine, suggesting that only those "unfortunate enough to have been born in Russia or Roumania [*sic*]" would consider such an impractical scheme.[40] Another article, from July 1899, maintained that Zionism fueled antisemitism because Zionists echoed anti-semites in their assertion that Jews do not belong in the nations of their birth.[41]

ALFRED DREYFUS

Unsurprisingly, given its hostility to Jewish nationalism, the *American Israelite* opposed attempts by American Jewish groups to intervene collectively in the Dreyfus Affair. When the *Forverts*, New York's Yiddish daily, on the eve of the Rennes trial proposed taking up a collection to present Dreyfus with a gold sword on behalf of American Jewry, an editorial in the *American Israelite* called the idea "idiotic." "The Jews have no especial interest in Dreyfus personally," the editor claimed, despite the fact that the *American Israelite* fed precisely such interest with its voluminous coverage of the affair targeted at an exclusively Jewish readership.[42] On the same page, it dismissed calls to form a "Hebrew Citizens League" to resist antisemitic persecution in the United States. And when reports of the Rennes verdict arrived on Yom Kippur, the newspaper approvingly cited the sermon of a reform rabbi in Detroit opposing "indignation meetings and so-called boycotts" of France in response to the news.[43]

Whereas the antisemitism unleashed by the Dreyfus Affair had posed a challenge to the editors of the *American Israelite* as they struggled to maintain their faith that Jews could thrive in Western liberal democracies, Dreyfus's vindication gave them a reason to celebrate. "The Jews of the world owe an inestimable debt of gratitude to the brave Frenchman," proclaimed an editorial in the newspaper in July 1906, after the exoneration, rejoicing that the affair definitively showed "that nothing was gained by any country, any people, any class, through race or religious prejudice."[44] The *American Israelite* was quick to draw conclusions meant to reassure its integrated readership: "The rehabilitation of Dreyfus can be viewed from many standpoints, political, military, social, and religious," the editor wrote. "To the [*American*] *Israelite* the 'triumph of virtue,' as the French press call it, means the beginning of the end of political anti-Semitism in France."[45] Although the happy news from France shared the page with reports on "The Horrors of Bialystok" and other accounts of antisemitism on the rise in Eastern Europe, the readers of the

148

American Israelite could at least breathe a sigh of relief that a civilized nation such as France had returned to its senses.[46]

In 1906, after Dreyfus had been exonerated and received the Legion of Honor, the *American Israelite* reflected again upon the case, underscoring that Dreyfus's rehabilitation had not come about through any sort of Jewish collective action: "the vindication of Major Dreyfus was not due to the solidarity of Jews as Jews," an editorial declared. On the contrary, the honor goes to France itself, which had seen its error and rectified it, thus demonstrating the continued viability of the liberal, integrationist model.[47] France had momentarily strayed, they argued, but ultimately returned to its liberal values. The last articles about the affair in the *American Israelite* touched on the political consequences of the case, including the Combes law separating church and state in France. As if to hammer home that Dreyfus's vindication also represented a vindication for the integrationists, the newspaper congratulated Joseph Reinach on his reelection to the French Legislative Assembly and celebrated "the numerous appointments of Jews to prominent places" in the French government. All's well that ends well, the *American Israelite* concluded.[48]

SOCIALISTS

Along with Zionism and integrationism, many Jews in the late nineteenth century turned to Socialism, and its promise of the international solidarity of the working class, as a solution to the "Jewish Question." Individual Jewish intellectuals had been drawn to the Socialist movement from its inception: Karl Marx himself was born Jewish, as were other early Socialist leaders like Ferdinand Lassalle. The increasing impoverishment of Jews in the Russian empire over the course of the nineteenth century, coupled with their demographic explosion, had made the prospect of Socialism especially appealing to the Eastern European Jewish masses by the 1890s. Some joined the various social democratic parties. Others became revolutionaries or gravitated to radical forms of anarchism. The large-scale immigration of Russian Jews in response to the pogroms of the 1880s meant that pockets of Yiddish-speaking Socialists could be found in major capitals throughout the world, including Paris, London, and especially New York City, by the time of the affair.

But if Socialism attracted many Jews, its appeal was not uncomplicated. A long tradition of Socialist antisemitism associated Jews with the capitalist enemy. Marx had called Judaism a religion of "huckstering" that worshipped the "worldly God" of money, and his disciple Pierre-Joseph Proudhon had gone so far as to call for the expulsion of Jews from France in the 1840s. Moreover, the internationalism of the Socialist movement, its exclusive emphasis on class solidarity, meant that Socialists tended to frown upon overt expressions of Jewish identity, even when such expressions were secular rather than religious. As a result, the various European Socialist parties were slow to respond to the rise of antisemitism in the 1880s and 1890s, often dismissing outbreaks of violence against Jews with assurances that such animosities were a by-product of capitalism and would disappear after the Socialist revolution.

The Dreyfus affair brought these tensions to a head. The French Socialist movement, already divided into several factions, split further over whether to take a stand for Dreyfus. We have seen that the hard-line Socialists, under the leadership of Jules Guesde, considered the affair a bourgeois conflict and hence of no concern to their working-class constituents, while Jean Jaurès broke with his Socialist comrades in early 1898 to became one of the leading Dreyfusards. His decisive intervention on behalf of the Jewish officer, and his outspoken opposition to antisemitism, helped ensure that a large section of the Socialist left in France would remain relatively free from antisemitism into the twentieth century.[49]

During the decade of the 1890s, France drew many working-class Jewish immigrants from Eastern Europe. Michael Marrus estimates that there were roughly twenty thousand Jewish workers in Paris at the time of the affair, many of whom were avidly Socialist and did not share the integrationist ideals of their native-born co-religionists. And if at first they were attracted to the internationalism of the Socialist movement with its emphasis on the solidarity of the working class regardless of race or religion—which was its own form of integrationism—they quickly grew frustrated by Socialist Party leaders' refusal to defend Dreyfus or speak out against antisemitism. The antisemitic riots following the publication of "J'Accuse" pushed them to take a stand.

In 1898, shortly after Jaurès's about-face, a body calling itself the Group of Socialist Jewish Workers of Paris wrote an open letter to the French Socialist Party arguing that the Dreyfus Affair had ignited a dangerous form of antisemitism and that the Socialists were doing nothing to oppose it. The statement spoke in nationalist terms of the collective suffering of the Jews, "our people," and Michael Marrus argues that its authors were influenced by Bernard Lazare's recent turn from Socialist anarchism toward Zionism. Marrus states that it was probably this same group that organized a protest meeting for Jewish workers at the time of the Rennes verdict, in September 1899, the only such Jewish protest meeting held in France during the affair. The announcement for the meeting in *Les Droits de l'homme*, a Dreyfusard newspaper, indicated that they were taking this step because the French Socialist Party had been unresponsive to their needs.[50]

If the affair pushed immigrant Socialists toward Jewish nationalism, it also caused certain native-born French Jews from bourgeois families to embrace the Socialist movement. The editors at *L'Univers israélite* even complained in 1899 that "the Dreyfus Affair has led a number of our co-religionists to socialism."[51] One of the most prominent among these young recruits was Léon Blum, who became a close follower of Jaurès during the affair. In *Souvenirs sur l'Affaire*, Blum described wanting to universalize the lessons of the crisis, to "move from the injustice done to an individual to social injustice more broadly."[52] According to Pierre Birnbaum, the Dreyfus Affair proved clarifying for Blum because it brought the divisions in the Socialist movement to the surface. Blum's brand of Socialism, derived from Jaurès, was humanitarian rather than revolutionary. It did not seek the overthrow of bourgeois governments, but rather to work within the French republican framework to achieve reform. He later put this brand of Socialism into practice as prime minister in the late 1930s, instituting such reforms as the forty-hour work week.[53]

The schism within the French Socialist Party between Guesde and Jaurès over Dreyfus had repercussions for Socialists around the world. In the Russian empire, the General Jewish Labor Bund had been founded in 1897 in Vilna (present-day Vilnius, Lithuania) as a secular Jewish workers' party to promote both Socialism and the rights of Yiddish-speaking Jews in the Russian empire. Bund leaders were skeptical of Guesde's brand of militant internationalism, which they thought neglected the needs of Jews. But the Bund also looked askance at the budding Zionist movement because of its efforts to enlist the aid of imperialist governments as well as Jewish bankers, such as the Rothschilds, in its plan to establish Jewish settlements in Palestine. The Bundists of the Russian empire closely watched developments in France. According to Jonathan Frankel, the Dreyfus Affair served as a crucial catalyst pushing the Bund to "once and for all mark itself off from the assimilationist tradition in socialism." This meant advocating for Jewish autonomy within the Russian empire, which the Bund officially adopted as its platform in 1901.[54]

Frankel describes how the Jewish Socialists in Russia were influenced by their comrades abroad, especially by the increas-

ingly powerful Yiddish press in New York. Home to an explod-
ing population of Jewish immigrants, New York had a handful
of Yiddish newspapers in the early 1890s. The most significant
of these was *Dos Abend Blatt* (The Evening Sheet), the mouth-
piece of the Socialist Labor Party of America, under the auto-
cratic direction of Daniel De Leon. Born in Curaçao to a Dutch
family of likely Sephardic origin, De Leon was, like his model
Jules Guesde, a die-hard internationalist who rejected the idea
of a specifically Jewish labor movement. The Dreyfus Affair
would cause a major rebellion against this party line.[55]

The origin of the rift went back to January 1897, when a
group of Socialist journalists split off from *Dos Abend Blatt* to
form their own paper, the *Forverts*. They were led by a charismatic immigrant journalist and novelist named Abraham Cahan,
who objected to the dictatorial methods of De Leon. Although
he eventually edited the *Forverts* for decades, Cahan initially left
the newly founded newspaper after a short time to write about
Jewish topics in various English-language publications. Several
of his pieces, which straddle the line between reportage and
fiction, focused on the Dreyfus Affair and in many ways anticipated Sholem Aleichem's "Dreyfus in Kasrilevke" in their
evocation of the Jewish obsession with the case.[56]

In Cahan's "Dreyfus and Haman," published in the *Com-
mercial Advertiser* on September 1, 1898, the narrator acts as an
ear on the street, spying on the Jews of the Lower East Side as
they talk of nothing but the affair: "The names of every actor
in the Dreyfus case, from the unhappy prisoner of Devil's Island himself down to the assistant of the lawyers on either side,
are well known, therefore, to every *cheder* [school] boy in the
ghetto, and when yesterday's news of the colonel's confession
burst upon the crowded streets of the Jewry, the name Henry
was caught up as that of an old acquaintance, and was accompanied by curses such as none but a ghetto market woman could
invent." While some of the Lower East Side immigrant Jews

argue that such an injustice could never happen in America, and others praise France for getting so worked up on behalf of a Jew, the last word in the piece belongs to a man who declares that Jews will only know true justice when the Messiah comes. Another Cahan piece, entitled "A Dreyfus Crank and a Pious Lutheran Widow," published the following week, describes a young immigrant Jew who falls in love with a gentile woman because she shares his fascination with the case. In "The Captain Before His Judges," published in *Harper's Weekly* on September 23, 1899, Cahan evoked the desolation of a Jewish congregation when they learn of the Rennes verdict on Yom Kippur. "'When, oh when, will come the end to our exile?'" the rabbi laments, his voice choked with sobs at the fate of Dreyfus.[57]

The editors who temporarily replaced Cahan at the *Forverts* shared his understanding of the sympathy for Dreyfus among the Jewish masses, and they would use this knowledge to drive a stake through the heart of their rivals at *Dos Abend Blatt*. Unsurprisingly, *Dos Abend Blatt* had followed Guesde in remaining detached from the affair, often mocking the efforts of the Dreyfusards. Typical headlines read "A Death Blow to Dreyfus" and "The Dreyfusards in Confusion." In contrast, the editors at the *Forverts* took a passionate and partisan interest in the affair, following Jaurès by adopting the cause of the Jewish officer as their own. Headlines proclaimed optimistically "Justice for Dreyfus," "Dreyfus's Innocence," and "Antisemites Defeated." Indeed, so strong was the *Forverts*'s identification with Dreyfus that the Socialist principles of the journal seemed at times to give way to a form of ethnic nationalism.[58]

To be sure, the editors of the *Forverts* used their voluminous coverage of the case to criticize the corruption of French republican institutions—the government bureaucracy, the judiciary, and especially the military.[59] But the editors knew that their readers took an interest in the case not because it offered proof of the decadence of bourgeois liberalism but because Dreyfus was a

Jew. Accordingly, the coverage in the *Forverts* played up the affair's sentimental side, with puff pieces devoted to Lucie and to the suffering of the prisoner on Devil's Island, which catered to the ethnic passions of their readership. They referred to Dreyfus as a tragic hero and showed an intimate concern for the details of his health. The illustrations of Dreyfus, Zola, and other heroes of the affair that often accompanied these articles were no doubt meant to appeal to as wide an audience as possible, including the marginally literate.[60]

Like the leaders of the Bund, whom they supported, the editors of the *Forverts* realized that the Yiddish-speaking masses felt an instinctive bond of solidarity with other Jews. This bond might be characterized as national in the sense that it expressed a feeling of belonging to the Jewish people. But the connection that the Jewish masses felt to Dreyfus—whether on the streets of Kasrilevke, Paris, or the Lower East Side—was so strong it felt almost familial. The *Forverts* realized that exploiting this bond, even if it meant soft-pedaling on political issues, would boost circulation.

Dos Abend Blatt never recovered from the ill will it inspired with its cynical coverage of the affair. It folded a few years later. The *Forverts*, meanwhile, continued to broaden its appeal by covering a range of cultural matters of interest to the Jewish community and courting readers of varied political ideologies. By 1912, its circulation reached 120,000. By the 1930s, at its peak, it had become one of the largest dailies in the United States, with a circulation approaching 275,000. The Dreyfus Affair was key to bringing about this transformation.[61]

It is striking that proponents of the three major Jewish political ideologies—the Zionists, the integrationists, and the Socialists—all found in the Dreyfus Affair confirmation of their answers to the "Jewish Question" despite the fact that their ideologies were in many ways diametrically opposed. This was because of the complexity of the affair, its many different phases.

The integrationists could fixate on Dreyfus's exoneration as the ultimate validation for their worldview, conveniently forgetting the antisemitic riots that preceded it. The Zionists could do the reverse, while Socialists could see in the affair the need for a specifically Jewish form of working-class solidarity. And whereas ultra-orthodox Jews tended to side with the integrationists because of their greater antipathy toward Zionism and Socialism, some religious writers viewed the conclusion of the affair as a sign that Jews should stay out of politics altogether. The Hebrew-language newspaper *Kol Mahazike ha-dat* (The Voice of the Upholders of Religion), published in Lviv (Ukraine), used Dreyfus's exoneration to argue that Jews cannot trust even the most tolerant of countries: "Dreyfus in enlightened France, after the miracles and the wonders, is now afraid to wear the crown that he deserves." In the same article, the newspaper warned against the false promise of Zionism. For Jews across the ideological and religious spectrum, the affair provided the lens through which they viewed their future. A defining moment for Jews on the eve of the twentieth century, the affair served to clarify ideological positions, and to draw battle lines, before the Holocaust and the creation of the State of Israel rendered prior answers to the "Jewish Question" obsolete.[62]

It could also be argued, though, that the affair brought to the surface not just the ideological differences dividing Jews but also the common bond uniting them. Before the nineteenth century, Jews felt linked to other Jews throughout the world, but these ties were mainly religious (the experience of participating in the same rituals, being bound by the same laws) or national (being part of an ancient nation now dispersed). In the nineteenth century, such bonds melted away for many Jews, as secularism took hold and Jews began to feel a part of the countries in which they lived. But they were replaced by a new unifying force: the memory of—and ongoing fear of—antisemitic persecution. This was what came to define Jewish identity for many modern Jews.

It arguably remains the common denominator constituting Jewish identity today.

The Dreyfus Affair represents one of the key moments when this new identity took shape. Along with a series of earlier antisemitic crises—such as the Russian pogroms of 1881–1882— the affair forced Jews to reconsider the possibility of integration into the modern nation-state and to conceive new forms of Jewish collective political action in response to the threats they faced.[63] On a deeper level, the affair reminded Jews of their belonging to a people with a painful history. As the *Jewish Chronicle* put it during the affair, "Dreyfus does indeed but epitomize the travail and the sufferings which Israel himself—the man of sorrows—has borne almost from the first hour of his national birth passing from disaster to disaster, and martyrdom to martyrdom." The affair tapped into a shared understanding of the difficulties Jews faced in the past and as a result inspired them to feel a sense of solidarity with other Jews in the present.[64]

Turn-of-the-century Jews may have disagreed about almost everything having to do with Jewish life, from how to worship to the need for a Jewish state, but they could come together in shared sorrow as they read about the plight of the prisoner of Devil's Island, and they could rejoice together as the vindicated Jewish officer received the Legion of Honor. It was in the collective experience of the affair and its precursors that a new Jewish "imagined community" took shape, beyond national, ideological, or religious borders. What Sholem Aleichem understood so well was that if the obsession with Dreyfus made the distance between Kasrilevke and Paris melt away, it was because the affair had helped to redefine the nature of Jewish identity for the modern age.[65]

7

The Aftermath

WHEN THE MINISTER OF WAR, Eugène Étienne, filed the paperwork to reinstate Dreyfus in the military in 1906, he recommended that the Jewish officer be promoted to the rank of major (*chef d'escadron*), whereas other officers of Dreyfus's generation had obtained this rank as early as 1901. Dreyfus was thus made subordinate to nearly a hundred officers with less seniority, which he understood to be a gesture of deference to the large contingent of anti-Dreyfusards within the army's ranks. The fact that his defender Picquart was promoted two full ranks to brigadier general in recognition of his role during the affair added insult to injury.[1]

The affair officially came to an end with Dreyfus's exoneration. But as the Dreyfusards realized, the fight was far from over. The struggle between two competing visions of France—one that would grant religious and racial minorities full equality and the other that would exclude them—continued to rage

throughout the twentieth century. In many ways, this same conflict continues to divide France today.

The new government that came to power on October 25,
1906, represented the triumph of the Dreyfusard coalition. Clemenceau became President of the Council (prime minister) and
Picquart was appointed minister of war. If Dreyfus at first hoped
that these two former supporters would rectify the latest injustice inflicted on him by the military authorities, he soon realized his mistake. Clemenceau had opposed Dreyfus's decision
to accept the pardon in 1899 and showed no inclination to help
him now. Picquart received Dreyfus cordially in his grand new
office at the ministry on November 29, 1906, but became "gla-
cial" when Dreyfus explained the reason for his visit. The decision to appoint him at the rank of major had been made by the
previous government, Picquart explained, and there was nothing he could do to change it. Although he did not believe this
explanation, Dreyfus understood that it was "useless to insist"
and quickly terminated the meeting.[2]

Rather than compromise his dignity, Dreyfus resigned from
the army on June 26, 1907. The military career that he had
dreamed of since he was a boy, and for which he had suffered
untold torments, came to an end. To a friend he wrote, "I prefer
to withdraw, my head held high, with sadness I will admit, but
at least with the satisfaction of having accomplished, everywhere
and always, my duty." Dreyfus was now a civilian for the first
time in twenty-seven years.[3]

Thanks to the continued prosperity of the family textile
firm, Dreyfus could devote his remaining years to reading, writing, and reflection. He worked on his memoirs and other proj-
ects, including writing book reviews for scholarly journals. After
all that he had suffered, he was more than happy to live a quiet,
domestic life, devoting himself to those he loved. "There was not
a trace of banality in that man, who scorned worldly conven-
tions and prejudices," one friend wrote. "Only his intimates could

fully appreciate the charm of his nature, its hidden treasure of goodness, rectitude, and affection."[4]

In the years that followed, Dreyfus took an active role in his children's education. After graduating from the Lycée Condorcet, Pierre attended the Collège Chaptal, where his father had prepared for the entrance exam to the École polytechnique, the training ground for military officers. Fearing the antisemitism that pervaded both Polytechnique and the officer corps during the affair, Pierre opted instead for the École centrale des arts et manufactures, where he earned an engineering degree. Like other daughters of bourgeois families, his younger sister, Jeanne, attended a private finishing school in the neighborhood, where she studied literature and domestic arts, such as embroidery. Alfred and Lucie supplemented their children's studies by teaching Latin, German, and other subjects at home.[5]

It was Lucie alone who took charge of the children's Jewish education. She read the Bible with them and took the children with her to synagogue on holidays and the anniversaries of the death of family members. Dreyfus did not oppose this religious instruction. Although not a "believer," he wrote on Devil's Island that he was "a sympathetic witness to those who believe—I am aware of the moral beauty of faith."[6] Both children married Jews: Jeanne married Pierre Paul Lévy, a doctor, and Pierre married Marie Baur, the daughter of a banker. Their cousins also married within the faith, and even within the Dreyfusard coalition: Mathieu's daughter Marguerite (Magui) married Joseph Reinach's son Adolph (Ado).

Despite his determination to guard his privacy, Dreyfus remained a very public figure—a subject of intense fascination and controversy. He was relentlessly attacked by the nationalist and antisemitic press in France. *La Libre parole* had lost influence after Drumont departed as editor in 1898, but its role was filled by equally extreme right-wing journals, especially *L'Action française*, founded in 1899 in opposition to the ascendancy of the Dreyfusard left. Under the leadership of Charles Maurras, *L'Action française* embraced the full reactionary program, promoting royalism, xenophobic nationalism, conservative Catholicism—and virulent antisemitism, which often took the form of attacks on Dreyfus himself. This time, Dreyfus fought back. He fired off more than thirty-six letters to the editors of these journals, including twelve to *L'Action française* alone. When the journal refused to print his letters, he sued Maurras in court, supported by the Human Rights League. After a three-year legal battle, Dreyfus eventually won his case against *L'Action française* in 1911.[7]

Dreyfus's great defender Émile Zola died in 1902 of carbon monoxide poisoning—rumors circulated that he had been murdered by an anti-Dreyfusard stove-fitter who had plugged up his chimney. A few years later, when it was announced that Zola's body would be transferred to the Pantheon—an honor accorded to the nation's "great men," which Zola earned largely because of his role during the affair—*L'Action française* attempted to whip up outrage from the far right. "Patriotic students, who do not want France devoured alive by the Jew and the alien, we call on your energy," an article proclaimed. On the morning of June 4, 1908, soldiers held back the crowd screaming "Down with Zola! Down with Dreyfus!" in front of the Pantheon. As Dreyfus joined the line of dignitaries leaving the ceremony, a shot rang out. Struck in the arm, Dreyfus was carried to a nearby police station, and the assailant was captured.

The sixty-year-old would-be assassin, Louis-Anthelme Grégori, claimed at his trial that he intended his bullet as a "symbolic act" aimed not at Dreyfus but at Dreyfusism, the liberal values that had triumphed after the revision of the verdict. Despite the energetic testimony of both Alfred and Mathieu Dreyfus during the trial, the jury determined that Grégori acted out of passion, not premeditation, and acquitted him. "It is the revision of the revision," rejoiced Maurras.[8]

The ideological civil war that divided France in the wake of the affair subsided somewhat during World War I, as the various political factions temporarily put aside their differences in a "sacred union" to fight the common enemy. At the age of fifty-five, Dreyfus came out of retirement to serve as an artillery officer in the war. Stationed first in the fortified zone north of Paris, he described feeling a "profound emotion" when he learned that the French army had captured his native Mulhouse, which had remained under German occupation since 1870. The entire Dreyfus family, and their business, would now once again be French.[9]

Dreyfus's son Pierre, a second lieutenant, survived years in the trenches and fought at the battles of Mulhouse, the Marne, the Oise, Champagne, and Verdun. In 1917, Alfred Dreyfus reported to the front, where he fought alongside Pierre in the Nivelle offensive, in which the French lost nearly two hundred thousand troops. Back at home, Lucie and Jeanne both volunteered as nurses. By the time the war ended, Pierre Dreyfus had been promoted to captain and received the Croix de Guerre. Alfred Dreyfus was finally promoted from major to lieutenant colonel and attained a higher level in the Legion of Honor. Mathieu Dreyfus's son Émile and his son-in-law Ado Reinach died in the conflict along with nearly two million other young French men.[10]

After the war, Alfred returned to peaceful pursuits—mainly reading and stamp collecting. Wearing the rosette of the Legion of Honor in the buttonhole of his neatly tailored suit, his back growing increasingly stooped as the years went by, he would take daily walks in his neighborhood near the Parc Monceau and sometimes journeyed by bus or Métro to play bridge with other retired officers in the clubhouse of the Cercle Militaire. He enjoyed seeing films in the movie palaces on the Champs-Elysées. When his grandchildren visited the apartment on the rue des Renaudes on Sunday afternoons, Alfred would lead them into his study and entertain them by singing popular songs and

Alfred Dreyfus in his later years (Photo © MAHJ / Niels Forg)

examining stamps. Summers were spent with friends by the shores of Lake Geneva or in Italy. But despite all his attempts to put the past behind him, he never stopped suffering from horrific nightmares of his time on Devil's Island.[11]

Lucie, meanwhile, devoted her later years to Jewish philanthropy. As a volunteer for the Israelite Welfare Committee of Paris, she distributed aid to the tens of thousands of Jewish refugees who fled to Paris in the 1920s and 1930s from Nazi Germany and the countries it had invaded. If these victims of persecution saw France as a kind of promised land, it was in no small part because of the outcome of the Dreyfus Affair. As the philosopher Emmanuel Levinas put it, quoting his Lithuanian father: "A country that tears itself in two to save the honor of a little Jewish officer is a country we should go to immediately."[12]

However, these immigrants were not always welcomed with open arms, even by their fellow Jews. Some of the native-born French Israelites who offered them aid saw their manners as uncouth and worried that their presence would stir up antisemitism. Lucie's own hesitations about the immigrants resulted less from snobbery than from patriotism. Regarding the increasing number of refugees from Nazi Germany, she wrote: "From a Jewish and humanitarian point of view, I should help them, but from a French point of view, I have a hard time extending a hand to our former enemies." Her son Pierre was less ambivalent. He served as the head of the Committee for the Defense of Jews Persecuted in Germany and volunteered on behalf of poor Eastern European Jewish refugees.[13]

Although Dreyfus did not play a public role in his later years, he kept abreast of current events. After his return from Devil's Island, Dreyfus befriended the Marquise Arconati-Visconti, the society hostess who had held one of the most important Dreyfusard salons during the affair, and attended her influential Thursday evening gatherings for several decades, where he encountered republican statesmen, such as Reinach, Jaurès, and Combes, along with a smattering of significant academics, journalists, and novelists. Dreyfus's recently published correspondence with the marquise, which stretches from 1899 to her death in 1923, reveals a curiosity and passion for ideas that he rarely revealed in public or even in his letters to Lucie. It also reveals a man with a profound—and at times surprising—set of political convictions.[14]

Rare for the son of a wealthy textile manufacturer, or for an army officer, Dreyfus took a sympathetic interest in the labor movement, even delivering lectures on the subject.[15] Although his views on the social question were not untinged by bourgeois paternalism, he expressed empathy for the suffering of the working class, which he directly linked to his own suffering on Devil's Island. "I am not a socialist," he wrote, "in the sense that I am not a collectivist, but I believe that people who struggle and work have a right to their share of happiness, and that we must strive to give it to them." At a time of anarchist bombings, when many members of the bourgeoisie closed ranks against the threat from below, Dreyfus supported the workers' right to strike and to engage in collective bargaining.[16]

He also took an interest in the "Jewish Question." In 1902, Herzl's newspaper *Die Welt* published an article by Dreyfus titled "Thoughts on Zionism," which expressed hope that the Jewish people would resist both annihilation by their enemies and disappearance through assimilation.[17] Although Dreyfus's remarks were noncommittal concerning the Zionist project, the editors of the journal noted that "one can quite clearly read from their tenor that Dreyfus is currently heading in our direction."[18] This was an exaggeration. Dreyfus displayed a clear understanding of the causes of antisemitism, but while not opposed to Zionism as a solution for Eastern European Jews, he retained his faith in the French republican model of integration. In 1926, Dreyfus joined the honorary committee of the newly established Accueil Fraternel Israélite (Israelite Fraternal Welcome), dedicated to helping to integrate refugee Jews in France.[19]

Although Dreyfus had returned from Devil's Island weak and frail, his hair white, he recovered sufficiently to see the birth of eight grandchildren. By the 1920s, though, he began to suffer from a series of urological ailments. In 1934, on vacation in Switzerland, he was rushed to a clinic and then back to Paris for emergency prostate surgery, after which he developed uremic poisoning. "When sickness laid him low, he never complained," wrote Pierre, who visited him daily as his health declined over the course of the next year. On July 11, 1935, Dreyfus held his son's hand longer than usual, without speaking, but communicating nevertheless "his final thoughts." He died the next day, at the age of seventy-five, surrounded by his family.[20]

His grandson, Jean-Louis Lévy, would write that when visiting his grandfather on his deathbed, he wondered about the evident sadness that lay behind his kind blue eyes—a sadness that we recognize today in every photograph of Dreyfus's later years. It was the result, Lévy eventually understood, of the "secret wound" of knowing that so many of his countrymen saw him as a symbol of treachery, the worst crime he could imagine. It was a knowledge he could not bear, but that he nevertheless endeavored to live with, day after day, for decades.

His funeral took place, fittingly, on Bastille Day, in the Jewish section of Montparnasse Cemetery, not far from the grave of Captain Armand Mayer, who had been killed in a duel defending the honor of Jewish officers fifty years before. In contrast to the very public commemorations following the death of Mayer and the various Dreyfusard heroes such as Zola, Dreyfus had a small ceremony, attended only by the immediate family and the Chief Rabbi, who recited the Kaddish prayer and lamented that the nation had seemingly forgotten the heroic sacrifice he had made.[21] But the scale of the funeral reflected the modesty of the man, who had always turned inward and whose very public life had been lived in spite of his desires and inclinations.

In its coverage of the death, which it buried on page two, *L'Action française* claimed falsely that by accepting the pardon in 1899, Dreyfus had acknowledged his guilt, and castigated both Dreyfus and his supporters for seeking to discredit the army.[22] The left-leaning papers largely refrained from using the occasion of Dreyfus's death to reflect on the larger meaning of the affair. *Le Temps* bent over backward to acknowledge the feelings of both sides, those who "took [Dreyfus] for the despised type of the soldier who betrayed his country and those who took him for a great martyr." "Today, and for a long time now, there is peace," they noted rather optimistically.[23] A few books appeared in the months that followed, including most notably *Souvenirs sur l'Affaire* by Léon Blum, who attempted to use the lesson of the affair to warn of the Nazi threat, but who wrongly cast Dreyfus himself as incapable of understanding the true import of his struggle.[24]

Despite the wishes of *Le Temps*, the fundamental conflict embodied by the Dreyfus Affair—over liberalism, universalism, and the place of minorities in the French nation—was rarely far from the surface of French consciousness in the 1930s. Shortly before becoming prime minister in 1936, Blum was dragged from a car and beaten almost to death by members of the Camelots du Roi, a proto-fascist antisemitic group under the umbrella of *L'Action française*. When Blum assumed power on June 6, 1936, announcing a number of labor reforms such as the forty-hour work week and paid vacations, Xavier Vallat, an extreme right-wing deputy from the Ardèche, rose to speak in the Chamber: "Your accession to power, Mr. Prime Minister, is undeniably a historic date. For the first time, this old Gallo-Roman country will be governed . . . by a Jew." After protests subsided, Vallat continued his diatribe: "In order to govern a peasant nation like France, it is better to have someone whose origins, modest though they may be, lie deep in the entrails of our soil, rather than a subtle Talmudist." As *L'Action française* put it: "the government of Léon Blum puts the Jewish question before the French people for the first time since the Dreyfus Affair."[25]

Kept out of power for decades as a result of the affair, the reactionary right got its revenge after France capitulated to Germany in 1940. The country divided into two zones: the North, including Paris, was directly occupied by Germany, while the South, with a capital at Vichy, remained nominally a "free zone" but in reality collaborated closely with the Nazis. Marshal Philippe Pétain, the aging World War I hero who became leader of the Vichy state, put in place an authoritarian, antiparliamentary, and antisemitic government of "National Revolution" that was everything the anti-Dreyfusards had dreamed. Vallat became the Commissioner-General for Jewish Questions and helped institute policies that effectively put an end to 150 years of Jewish equality in France. Jews were stripped of their rights, driven from their jobs and homes, and eventually rounded up by French police. During the war, one in four Jews on French soil—nearly 75,000 people—were deported to death camps in Poland and murdered. Despite already having suffered so much, the Dreyfus family was not spared the horror.

Like many other native-born French Jews, the Dreyfuses had the means to flee Paris in June 1940 ahead of the Nazi invasion. Lucie, seventy-one years old, joined her children and grandchildren and headed south by car, on roads packed with refugees. Although French Jews had not yet been forced to register with the police—a measure that would later aid in rounding them up—the family rightly believed that their notoriety would make them targets for the Nazis. Shortly after their departure, Pierre's home was raided by the Gestapo, which wanted to shut down the operations of Jewish welfare groups, including those that Pierre worked for. While Pierre and his family headed first to Marseilles and then to the Upper West Side in Manhattan, Lucie and Jeanne's family sheltered in Toulouse.

Lucie spent the next two years shuttling among various relatives in the south of France, staying in boarding houses and hotels. She had brought a quantity of cash with her when she fled Paris, but soon began to run out of money. After the Nazis put an end to the Vichy government in 1942 and all of France became an occupied zone, Lucie took on a false name. During the affair, she had often used her in-laws' name, Valabrègue, to disguise her identity, but this was almost as obviously Jewish a name to French ears as Dreyfus. She now took the more generic name Duteil and hid in a Catholic convent in Valence for the remainder of the war. Her letters and notebooks from this time are filled with records of her reading—Spinoza, Nietzsche, and Gide, as well as books on Jewish literature and the Hebrew Bible. Whether the "good sisters of Valence" guessed the true identity of their erudite *Israélite* border, they kept her secret, and Lucie survived the war. She died, of natural causes, after the liberation, in December 1945.[26]

Other members of the family were not as fortunate. Her twenty-three-year-old granddaughter Madeleine Lévy, Alfred's favorite grandchild, fled to Toulouse with her family at the start of the war. A former member of a Jewish scouting organization, Madeleine had protested as a teenager against an antisemitic professor who insulted the memory of her grandfather, and she displayed this same rebellious spirit under occupation. In Toulouse, she began working for the Vichy-funded Secours National, a general welfare organization, but along with her siblings she secretly contributed to the French Resistance, helping Jewish refugees flee to Spain by providing them with counterfeit documents and food. Promoted to the grade of *adjutant* with the French Forces of the Interior, she was offered a position in Lyon with the resistance organization Combat. She was arrested on November 3, 1943, in Toulouse, as she packed some warm clothes for the winter.[27]

Instead of being sent to a detention camp for political prisoners, Madeleine was transferred, along with three other Jewish resistance fighters, to the Drancy camp north of Paris, where she joined three thousand other Jews, including several Dreyfus and Reinach cousins. "Do not concern yourself," she wrote to a friend on the outside. "I can be useful and help others through my vocation as a social worker." She would try to care for the eighty-three children under the age of twelve on Convoy 62, which departed Drancy for Auschwitz on November 20, 1943, packed with nearly twelve hundred Jews. After surviving the hellish three-day journey to Poland, and the first selection upon arrival, Madeleine was assigned number 69036 and admitted to the women's barracks at Birkenau. She withstood two months of grueling slave labor in the freezing cold but succumbed to typhus in January 1944. She was twenty-five years old.[28]

After the war, Xavier Vallat was sentenced to ten years for his collaboration with the Nazis, but served only two before being paroled in 1949 and amnestied in 1954. When Charles Maurras, the editor of *L'Action française*, was sentenced to life imprisonment for his collaboration, he declared, "It's the revenge of Dreyfus!" He served seven years before receiving a "medical pardon" shortly before his death in 1952.

Despite these efforts at amnesty, the conflict over the Dreyfus Affair has never really ended in France. In the run-up to the 2022 presidential election, the far-right candidate Éric Zemmour, a master of provocation, sparked a calculated outrage on the left by claiming that Dreyfus's innocence was "not obvious."[29] An Algeria-born Jew, Zemmour was vying with Marine Le Pen for the votes of the far right. Demonizing Dreyfus remains a potent dog whistle for this demographic. Le Pen, after all, is heir to the National Front, the party founded by her father Jean-Marie, whose motto "France for the French" (*La France aux Français*) was lifted from the masthead of *La Libre parole*. If the past continues to echo in France, often in shocking ways, it is because the issues raised by the Dreyfus Affair—raised because Dreyfus was a Jew—continue to be fought over with a passion that is as strong today as it was in the 1890s.

Dreyfus never intended to become a symbol of antisemitic persecution. A religious skeptic and a proud Frenchman, he never renounced his Jewish heritage, or tried to hide it, but he certainly never desired to become the face of the "Jewish Question," the very image of Jewish victimhood for some and of the Jewish enemy for others. His tomb in the crowded Jewish section of the Montparnasse Cemetery is a monument to this conflict at the heart of his identity. A sober gray slab, unadorned, the

Dreyfus family tomb at Montparnasse Cemetery

tomb contains merely a list of names, with that of Lieutenant Colonel Alfred Dreyfus at the top. Directly beneath his is the name of his favorite granddaughter, Madeleine Lévy, and under hers the names of Lucie, Pierre, and Jeanne, in order of their deaths. Dreyfus is identified only by his rank in the French military and by the qualification, "Officer of the Legion of Honor." There is no Hebrew lettering or symbol to identify this as a

Jewish tomb at all—except for the words, under the name of Madeleine, "Deported by the Germans, disappeared at Auschwitz." And the fact that, on the day I visited and in every picture of the tomb I have seen, the monument is covered by small stones left by visitors, in keeping with the Jewish custom of honoring the dead.

Introduction

1. Léon Lipschutz listed 551 works about the affair in *Une Bibliographie dreyfusienne: Essai de Bibliographie thématique et analytique de l'Affaire Dreyfus* (Paris: Fasquelle, 1970), and the number has grown exponentially since then.

2. Jean-Denis Bredin, *The Affair: The Case of Alfred Dreyfus*, trans. Jeffrey Mehlman (New York: George Braziller, 1983), 139. I discuss exceptions to the reticence by Jews to confront antisemitism in Chapters 2 and 3.

3. The few works about the affair that make antisemitism the focus include Stephen Wilson, *Ideology and Experience: Antisemitism in France at the Time of the Dreyfus Affair* (Liverpool: Liverpool University Press, 1982); and Pierre Birnbaum, *The Anti-Semitic Moment: A Tour of France in 1898*, trans. Jane Marie Todd (Chicago: University of Chicago Press, 2011). Bertrand Joly minimizes the role of antisemitism in the affair in *Histoire politique de l'affaire Dreyfus* (Paris: Fayard, 2014), 315–319. Vincent Duclert's excellent biography

Alfred Dreyfus: L'honneur d'un patriote (Paris: Fayard, 2006) downplays Dreyfus's Jewishness, a criticism made by Sudhir Hazareesingh in his review of the book: "The only regret that one might express is the absence of a more systematic analysis of the Jewish culture of the Dreyfuses" (*Cahiers Jaurès* 4:186 [2007], 19). One of the few books to focus on Dreyfus's Jewishness is Michael Burns, *Dreyfus: A Family Affair, 1780–1945* (New York: HarperCollins, 1991).

4. Vincent Duclert makes a similar argument in *Alfred Dreyfus: L'honneur d'un patriote*, new edition (2006; Paris: Fayard/Pluriel, 2016), 61. References to Duclert are to the 2016 edition unless otherwise stated.

5. Burns, *Dreyfus*, 401.

6. Louis Begley, *Why the Dreyfus Affair Matters* (New Haven: Yale University Press, 2009).

Chapter 1. The Soldier

1. Burns, *Dreyfus*, 4.

2. Burns, *Dreyfus*, 3.

3. Phyllis Cohen Albert, *The Modernization of French Jewry: Consistory and Community in the Nineteenth Century* (Waltham, Mass.: Brandeis University Press, 1977), 24.

4. Odile Jurbert, *Dreyfus avant Dreyfus: Une famille juive de Mulhouse* (Mulhouse: Imp. Ville de Mulhouse, 1994), 14–15, 30–31.

5. Thomas A. Sancton, "The Myth of French Worker Support for the North in the American Civil War," *French Historical Studies* 11:1 (Spring 1979), 58–80; Burns, *Dreyfus*, 35–36; Jurbert, *Dreyfus avant Dreyfus*, 9.

6. Jurbert, *Dreyfus avant Dreyfus*, 18.

7. Jurbert, *Dreyfus avant Dreyfus*, 24.

8. In certain official documents, including the census of 1866, Jeannette used the name Adèle Weill, a patronym adopted by her father. The patronyms of Jews often fluctuated in this period. Jurbert, *Dreyfus avant Dreyfus*, 23.

9. Burns, *Dreyfus*, 40–42.

10. H. Villemar [Hélène Naville], *Dreyfus intime* (Paris: Stock, 1898), 7–8.

11. In *La Vraie Vie du Capitaine Dreyfus* (Paris: Tallandier, 2014), Laurent Greilsamer claims that Dreyfus celebrated his bar mitzvah in Carpentras, while visiting his sister (20). However, I have found no other reference to such a ceremony, and no record of it exists in the Carpentras synagogue archive. On Jewish education in Mulhouse, see Jeffrey Haus, *Challenges of Equality: Judaism, State, and Education in Nineteenth-Century France* (Detroit: Wayne State University Press, 2009), 59.

12. See Alfred Dreyfus, *Cinq années de ma vie* (Paris: Maspero, 1982), 57; also cited in Burns, *Dreyfus*, 51.

13. Dreyfus describes his hatred of Germany in a letter to the minister of war (Bibliothèque Nationale, nouvelle acquisitions françaises [BN, NAF] 16464, December 25, 1897); also cited in Burns, *Dreyfus*, 52.

14. Alfred Dreyfus, *Souvenirs et correspondance, publiés par son fils* (Paris: Grasset, 1936), 41.

15. Burns, *Dreyfus*, 61–62; Duclert, *Alfred Dreyfus*, 72.

16. Duclert, *Alfred Dreyfus*, 73.

17. Villemar, *Dreyfus intime*, 9–10.

18. Burns, *Dreyfus*, 64–65; Duclert, *Alfred Dreyfus*, 74. Dreyfus reflected on his school days in BN, NAF 24909, 1898–99, notebook 217.

19. Villemar, *Dreyfus intime*, 10.

20. Derek J. Penslar, *Jews and the Military: A History* (Princeton: Princeton University Press, 2013), 86–96. Also see Pierre Birnbaum, *The Jews of the Republic: A Political History of State Jews in France from Gambetta to Vichy*, trans. Jane Marie Todd (Stanford: Stanford University Press, 1996), especially 179–198.

21. Duclert, *Alfred Dreyfus*, 78.

22. Penslar, *Jews and the Military*, 96.

23. Penslar, *Jews and the Military*, 86; Duclert, *Alfred Dreyfus*, 80–81.

24. Duclert, *Alfred Dreyfus*, 81.

25. Sander Gilman, "The Jewish Voice," in *The Jew's Body* (New York: Routledge, 1991), 10–37.

26. Duclert, *Alfred Dreyfus*, 82.

27. Duclert, *Alfred Dreyfus*, 85; Burns, *Dreyfus*, 74–75.

28. On Dreyfus's liaisons, see Duclert, *Alfred Dreyfus*, 100. On his attraction to Lucie, see Villemar, *Dreyfus intime*, 13, and Dreyfus, *Cinq années*, 58.

29. The Jewish newspaper *Les Archives israélites* published an obituary when she died in 1843: page 292 of the consecutively paginated newspaper for that year.

30. Duclert, *Alfred Dreyfus*, 90.

31. Hannah Arendt, *The Origins of Totalitarianism* (1968; New York: Harvest, 1976), 103.

32. Arendt, *Origins of Totalitarianism*, 117.

33. Michael Marrus, *The Politics of Assimilation: A Study of the French Jewish Community at the Time of the Dreyfus Affair* (Oxford: Clarendon Press, 1971), 2.

34. Cited in Marrus, *Politics of Assimilation*, 90–91.

35. Moïse Schuhl, "La Patrie juive," *L'Univers israélite* 24, September 1, 1886, 755–759.

36. Dreyfus, *Souvenirs et correspondance*, 51.

37. Arnaud Aron and Jonas Ennery, *Prières d'un coeur israélite, livre d'offices et receuil de prières et de méditations pour toutes les circonstances de la vie, publié par la Société consistoriale des bons livres*, 3rd edition (Paris: A. Kaufmann, 1861).

38. Joseph Reinach, *Histoire de l'affaire Dreyfus*, vol. 1 (Paris: Robert Laffont, 2006), 399.

39. Mathieu Dreyfus's daughter Magui, whose first husband, Ado Reinach, was killed in World War I, became the first family member to marry a non-Jew in 1927. Burns, *Dreyfus*, 411.

40. Ruth Harris makes a similar point about the persistence of Jewish culture in the Dreyfus family in *Dreyfus: Politics, Emotion, and the Scandal of the Century* (New York: Metropolitan, 2010), 66–67. David Sorkin describes the "subculture" of German Jews in *The Transformation of German Jewry, 1780–1840* (Detroit: Wayne State University Press, 1999).

41. "Dreyfus represented according to the examining magistrate an ideal target because he didn't hide his origins, because he was not a self-hating Jew who hid the fact that he was Jewish." Bau-

douin, Réquisitoire, Réhabilitation, 1903–1906, Débats 1906, I, 370, cited in Duclert, *Alfred Dreyfus*, 543.

42. Burns, *Dreyfus*, 98. Duclert criticizes recent historians for repeating subjective assessments of Dreyfus's personality from the time of the affair; Duclert, *Alfred Dreyfus*, 25.

43. Archives nationales BB/19/128; *Cour de Cassation: Enquête de la chambre criminelle: Affaire Dreyfus: 2e revision* (Paris: Imprimerie Nationale, 1905), 434, discussed in Duclert, *Alfred Dreyfus*, 145–146.

Chapter 2. The Arrest

1. Duclert, *Alfred Dreyfus*, 113.
2. Duclert, *Alfred Dreyfus*, 96; Villemar, *Dreyfus intime*, 15.
3. Dreyfus, *Cinq années*, 60.
4. Duclert, *Alfred Dreyfus*, 41.
5. Nancy Fitch describes the antisemitism of the rural population during the Dreyfus Affair in "Mass Culture, Mass Parliamentary Politics and Anti-Semitism," *American Historical Review* 97:1 (February 1992), 55–95.
6. Shulamit Volkov, "Antisemitism as a Cultural Code: Reflections on the History and Historiography of Antisemitism in Imperial Germany," *Yearbook of the Leo Baeck Institute* 23 (1978), 25–45.
7. Édouard Drumont, *La France juive* (1886; Paris: Éditions du Trident, 1987), 1:ii.
8. Drumont, *La France juive*, 1:387.
9. Elisabeth Parinet, *La Librairie Flammarion, 1875–1914* (Paris: Imec, 1992), 256.
10. On antisemitic discourse in the 1880s, see Marc Angenot, *Ce que l'on dit des Juifs en 1889: Antisémitisme et discours social* (Saint-Denis: Presses Universitaires de Vincennes, 1989). On Catholic antisemitism, see Vicky Caron, "Catholic Political Mobilization and Anti-Semitic Violence in Fin-de-siècle France," *Journal of Modern History* 81:2 (June 2009), 294–346; and Michael R. Marrus, "Popular Anti-Semitism," in *The Dreyfus Affair*, ed. Norman Kleeblatt (Berkeley: University of California Press, 1987), 57–60. Also see

Michel Winock, *Édouard Drumont et Cie: Antisémitisme et fascisme en France* (Paris: Seuil, 1982).

11. Official Consistory figures list the Jewish population at 71,249, with an additional 45,000 Jews in Algeria in 1897. Marrus argues that this is an undercount ("Popular Anti-Semitism," 31).

12. P. de Lamase, "Les Juifs à l'armée," *La Libre parole*, May 23, 1892, 2.

13. De Lamase, "Les Juifs à l'armée," 2.

14. Salomon Reinach, *Drumont et Dreyfus: Études sur la "Libre Parole" de 1894 à 1895* (Paris: Stock, 1898), 7.

15. Marrus, *Politics of Assimilation*, 141. Arendt asserts that the desire for assimilation explains why there were "few wholehearted supporters of Dreyfus . . . in the ranks of French Jewry"; Arendt, *Origins of Totalitarianism*, 118.

16. Marrus, *Politics of Assimilation*, 148.

17. Ernest Crémieu-Foa, *La Campagne antisémitique. Les duels. Les responsabilités. Mémoire avec pièces justificatives* (Paris: Alcan-Lévy, 1892), 27.

18. Pierre Dreyfus, "La Vie du capitaine Dreyfus exposée par son fils," in Alfred Dreyfus, *Souvenirs et correspondance publiés par son fils*, 21.

19. "Le Dossier du Commandant Forzinetti," *Le Figaro*, November 21, 1897, 2.

20. Cited in Joseph Reinach, *Histoire de l'affaire Dreyfus*, 1:93.

21. Archives nationales, BB/19/75, dossier 4.

22. Penslar, *Jews and the Military*, 107.

23. Penslar, *Jews and the Military*, 101.

24. Duclert, *Alfred Dreyfus*, 107.

25. Joseph Reinach, *Histoire de l'affaire Dreyfus*, 1:42.

26. Duclert, *Alfred Dreyfus*, 128.

27. Harris, *Dreyfus*, 19–20.

28. Cited in Marcel Thomas, *L'Affaire sans Dreyfus* (Paris: Arthème Fayard, 1971), 112.

29. Bredin, *The Affair*, 73.

30. Joseph Reinach, *Histoire de l'affaire Dreyfus*, 1:42.

31. Pierre Dreyfus, "La Vie du capitaine Dreyfus," 26.

32. Duclert, *Alfred Dreyfus*, 131.

33. Thomas, *L'Affaire sans Dreyfus*, 115. Eric Cahm makes a similar point in *The Dreyfus Affair in French Society and Politics* (London: Longman, 1996), 4.

34. Cited in Thomas, *L'Affaire sans Dreyfus*, 115.

35. Maurice Barrès, *Scènes et doctrines du nationalisme* (1902; Paris: Éditions du Trident, 1987), 112.

36. Cited in Thomas, *L'Affaire sans Dreyfus*, 114.

37. Cited in Duclert, *Alfred Dreyfus*, 48–49.

38. "Le Dossier du Commandant Forzinetti," 1.

39. Dreyfus, *Cinq années*, 62.

40. "Le Dossier du Commandant Forzinetti," 1. Also cited in Duclert, *Alfred Dreyfus*, 50.

41. Duclert, *Alfred Dreyfus*, 167.

42. Harris, *Dreyfus*, 27; Bredin, *The Affair*, 75–76.

43. Philippe Oriol, *Histoire de l'Affaire Dreyfus de 1894 à nos jours* (Paris: Belles lettres, 2014), 82.

44. *La Libre parole*, November 14, 1894, cited in Bredin, *The Affair*, 79.

45. Bredin, *The Affair*, 79.

46. Dreyfus, *Cinq années*, 66.

47. Dreyfus, *Cinq années*, 67.

48. Harris, *Dreyfus*, 30.

49. These insinuations were made by General de Dionne and are contained in piece 97 of the "dossier secret," preserved at the Musée d'art et d'histoire du Judaïsme (MAHJ), Fonds Dreyfus, 97.17.061.1.

50. Begley, *Why the Dreyfus Affair Matters*, 18.

51. Dreyfus, *Cinq années*, 71.

52. Archives nationales, BB/19/75, dossier 4.

53. Dreyfus, *Cinq années*, 72.

54. Dreyfus, *Cinq années*, 79–80.

55. Dreyfus, *Cinq années*, 81. The hand-drawn plan for the ceremony can be found in the Archives nationales, BB/19/75, dossier 4.

56. Dreyfus, *Cinq années*, 80.

57. Bredin, *The Affair*, 130. In their coverage of the event the following day, newspapers gave conflicting accounts: *Le Figaro* and *La Libre parole* reported cries of "Down with the Jews!" and "Dirty Jew!" emanating from the crowd outside the gates, while *Le Siècle* and *Le Temps*, along with the *New York Times*, did not report the word "Jew" being shouted.

58. Dreyfus, *Cinq années*, 81.

59. "Rapport du Lieutenant Colonel Guérin," Archives nationales, BB/19/75, dossier 4.

60. Harris, *Dreyfus*, 34; Bredin, *The Affair*, 105.

Chapter 3. The Prisoner

1. Dreyfus, *Cinq années*, 82; cited in Duclert, *Alfred Dreyfus*, 236; Burns, *Dreyfus*, 159.

2. Dreyfus, *Cinq années*, 92. Also see Jeanne Bernard-Grit, *Alfred Dreyfus en détention à l'île de Ré* (Saintes Mail, France: Le Croît Vif, 2017), 24.

3. Cited in Burns, *Dreyfus*, 164.

4. Burns, *Dreyfus*, 163; Begley, *Why the Dreyfus Affair Matters*, 21. Also see Stephen A. Toth, *Beyond Papillon: The French Overseas Penal Colonies, 1854–1952* (Lincoln: University of Nebraska Press, 2008), 17.

5. Many scholars (including Bredin, Burns, and Duclert) have described the conditions of Dreyfus's imprisonment. I draw from all their accounts as well as from Dreyfus's own writings.

6. The log books of the guards are preserved at the MAHJ, Fonds Dreyfus, 97.17.007.001-004.

7. Burns, *Dreyfus*, 168.

8. See, for example, Dreyfus's journal entries for April 24 and April 26, 1895, in *Cinq années*, 122.

9. Toth, *Beyond Papillon*, 131; also see Duclert, *Alfred Dreyfus*, 264.

10. Journal entry for April 14, 1895, in Dreyfus, *Cinq années*, 111, 114.

11. Burns, *Dreyfus*, 200.

12. Alfred and Lucie Dreyfus, *Écrire, c'est résister: Correspon-

dance (1894–1899), ed. Marie-Neige Coche and Vincent Duclert (Paris: Gallimard, 2019), 114.

13. Cited in Duclert, *Alfred Dreyfus*, 335.

14. Dreyfus, *Cinq années*, 107, 123.

15. Dreyfus, *Cinq années*, 133–134.

16. Duclert, *Alfred Dreyfus*, 61.

17. Dreyfus, *Cinq années*, 111, 157.

18. Dreyfus, *Cinq années*, 145–146.

19. Bredin, *The Affair*, 129.

20. Joseph Reinach, *Histoire de l'affaire Dreyfus*, 1:415.

21. Mathieu Dreyfus, *L'Affaire telle que je l'aie vécue* (Paris: Grasset, 1978), 20. Also cited in Philippe-E. Landau, *L'Opinion juive et l'affaire Dreyfus* (Paris: Albin Michel, 1995), 21.

22. Joseph Reinach, *Histoire de l'affaire Dreyfus*, 1:428.

23. *La Croix*, December 27, 1894; cited in Landau, *L'Opinion juive et l'affaire Dreyfus*, 34.

24. "Dossier secret," MAHJ, Fonds Dreyfus, 97.17.061.1, pièces 88 and 90.

25. Bredin, *The Affair*, 136; Joseph Reinach, *Histoire de l'affaire Dreyfus*, 1:434.

26. Emile Zola, "Pour les Juifs," in *L'Affaire Dreyfus: La Vérité en marche* (Paris: Flammarion, 1994), 57.

27. Bredin, *The Affair*, 137.

28. Robert S. Wistrich, "Max Nordau and the Dreyfus Affair," *Journal of Israeli History* 16:1 (1995), 9.

29. Charles Péguy, *Notre jeunesse* (Paris: Gallimard, 1993), 156.

30. Léon Blum, *Souvenirs sur l'Affaire* (1935; Paris: Gallimard, 1981), 42–43.

31. Blum, *Souvenirs*, 44.

32. Arendt, *Origins of Totalitarianism*, 10, 109.

33. Isidore Singer, "La Trahison du capitaine Alfred Dreyfus et la légende de solidarité juive," *La Vraie parole*, November 10, 1894, 1.

34. Marrus, *Politics of Assimilation*, 212–213.

35. Richard I. Cohen, "The Dreyfus Affair and the Jews," in *Antisemitism Through the Ages*, ed. Shmuel Almog (Oxford: Pergamon,

1980), 294. Also see Paula Hyman, "The French Jewish Community from Emancipation to the Dreyfus Affair," in *The Dreyfus Affair: Art, Truth, and Justice*, ed. Norman Kleeblatt (Berkeley: University of California Press), 31.

36. "Réaction salutaire," *Les Archives israélites* 45, November 8, 1894, 371.

37. Peloni, "Un Mouvement d'opinion," *Les Archives israélites* 50, December 13, 1894, 411.

38. Isidore Cahen, "Sommes-nous défendus?" *Les Archives israélites* 52, December 27, 1894, 423-424. On the reaction to the affair in the Jewish press, also see Cohen, "The Dreyfus Affair and the Jews," 297-299; and Landau, *L'Opinion juive et l'affaire Dreyfus*.

39. A.H. and L.W., "Encore Dreyfus," *L'Univers israélite*, January 16, 1895, 30.

40. Joseph Reinach, *Histoire de l'affaire Dreyfus*, 1:190.

41. Birnbaum, *The Jews of the Republic*, 84-85.

42. Perrine Simon-Nahum, "Zadoc Kahn, une figure du judaïsme français restée longtemps secrète," in *Être Dreyfusard hier et aujourd'hui*, ed. Gilles Manceron and Emmanuel Naquet (Rennes: Presses universitaires de Rennes, 2009), 131-134. Also see Stephen Wilson, *Ideology and Experience*, 716-717.

43. Philippe Oriol, "Zadoc Kahn et l'Affaire Dreyfus," in *Zadoc Kahn: Un grand rabbin entre culture juive, affaire Dreyfus et laïcité*, ed. Jean-Claude Kuperminc and Jean-Philippe Chaumont (Paris: Éditions de l'Éclat, 2007), 153-169.

44. Bredin, *The Affair*, 134.

45. On Bernard Lazare, see Nelly Wilson, *Bernard-Lazare and the Problems of Jewish Identity in Late Nineteenth-Century France* (Cambridge: Cambridge University Press, 2011); and Lauren Gottlieb Lockshin, "The Dreyfus Affair's Forgotten Hero: Bernard Lazare and the First Modern Fight Against Antisemitism," *Jewish History* 34 (2021), 305-330.

46. P.-V. Stock, *Mémorandum d'un éditeur: L'Affaire Dreyfus anecdotique* (Paris: Stock, 1938), 18; cited in Bredin, *The Affair*, 135.

47. Cited in Bredin, *The Affair*, 138.

48. Cited by Jean-Louis Lévy, "Alfred Dreyfus, anti-héros et témoin capital," postface in Alfred Dreyfus, *Cinq années*, 245; and Duclert, *Alfred Dreyfus*, 632.

49. Hannah Arendt, introduction to Bernard Lazare, *Job's Dungheap: Essays on Jewish Nationalism and Social Revolution*, trans. Harry Lorin Binsse (New York: Schocken, 1948), 9.

50. Zvi Jonathan Kaplan and Lauren Gottlieb Lockshin, "Silent or Outspoken? Re-Examining French Jewish Responses to the Dreyfus Affair," *Antisemitism Studies* 6:1 (Spring 2022), 4–31.

51. Nancy L. Green, *The Pletzl of Paris: Jewish Immigrant Workers in the Belle Époque* (New York: Holmes and Meier, 1986), 173.

Chapter 4. The Affair

1. Harris, *Dreyfus*, 49.

2. Translated in Bredin, *The Affair*, 143. Bredin's account of the climax of the affair remains one of the best, and I draw from it in this chapter.

3. Adam Gopnik, "Trial of the Century," *New Yorker*, September 28, 2009, 74.

4. Joseph Reinach, *Histoire de l'affaire Dreyfus*, 1:439–440.

5. Alfred Dreyfus, *Cinq années*, 166.

6. Bredin, *The Affair*, 169.

7. Translated in Bredin, *The Affair*, 173.

8. Bredin, *The Affair*, 174–175.

9. Maurice Paléologue, *My Secret Diary of the Dreyfus Case*, trans. Eric Mosbacher (London: Secker and Warburg, 1957), 57.

10. Blum, *Souvenirs*, 35–37.

11. Harris, *Dreyfus*, 7, 151–152.

12. Emile Zola, *L'Argent* (Paris: Gallimard Folio, 1980), 56.

13. Joseph Reinach, *Histoire de l'affaire Dreyfus*, 1:805; Stephen Wilson, *Ideology and Experience*, 330–335.

14. *Journal officiel de la République française, Débats parlementaires, Chambre des députés* (Paris: Imp. du Journal officiel, 1881–1940), January 24, 1898, p. 163. Also see Harvey Goldberg, "Jean Jaurès and the Jewish Question," *Jewish Social Studies* 20:2 (April 1958), 67–94.

15. Translated in Michael Burns, *France and the Dreyfus Affair: A Documentary History* (Boston: Bedford/St. Martin's, 1999), 119.

16. Harris, *Dreyfus*, 261–262; Duclert, *Alfred Dreyfus*, 493.

17. *La Libre parole*, January 12, 1898, translated in Birnbaum, *Anti-Semitic Moment*, 8.

18. *L'Echo de Paris*, January 12, 1898, translated in Birnbaum, *Anti-Semitic Moment*, 9.

19. Birnbaum, *Anti-Semitic Moment*, 9.

20. Michel Winock, "Les Deux France," in *L'Affaire Dreyfus*, ed. Michel Winock (Paris: Seuil, 1998), 145.

21. Birnbaum, *Anti-Semitic Moment*, 5.

22. Birnbaum, *Anti-Semitic Moment*, 11.

23. Birnbaum, *Anti-Semitic Moment*, 13, 14, 23–24.

24. Bredin, *The Affair*, 285–286. Also see a report on the anti-semitic riots in *Les Archives israélites*, January 27, 1898, 26.

25. Bredin, *The Affair*, 287.

26. Bredin, *The Affair*, 288.

27. Guy Chapman, *The Dreyfus Case: A Reassessment* (London: R. Hart-Davis, 1955), 28; cited in Paula Hyman, "New Perspectives on the Dreyfus Affair," *Historical Reflections/Réflexions historiques* 31:3 (2005), 336.

28. Bertrand Joly, *Histoire politique de l'affaire Dreyfus* (Paris: Fayard, 2014), 110, 315–319.

29. Fitch, "Mass Culture, Mass Parliamentary Politics and Anti-Semitism," 57; Joseph Reinach, *Histoire de l'affaire Dreyfus*, 1:1035.

30. Birnbaum, *Anti-Semitic Moment*, 4; Alfred Dreyfus, *Souvenirs et correspondance publiés par son fils* (Paris: Grasset, 1936), 227.

31. On the role of intellectuals during the affair, see Christophe Charle, *Birth of the Intellectuals, 1880–1900*, trans. David Fernbach and G. M. Goshgarian (Cambridge, U.K.: Polity, 2015). Also see Winock, *L'Affaire Dreyfus*, 145, and Bredin, *The Affair*, 276.

32. Herman Lebovics, *True France: The Wars over Cultural Identity, 1900–1945* (Ithaca: Cornell University Press, 1992), 7–8.

33. Susan Rubin Suleiman, "The Literary Significance of the Dreyfus Affair," in *The Dreyfus Affair*, ed. Kleeblatt, 118–119.

34. Linda Nochlin, "Degas and the Dreyfus Affair: A Portrait

of the Artist as an Anti-Semite," in *The Dreyfus Affair*, ed. Klee-blatt, 96.

35. Bredin, *The Affair*, 262.

36. Translated in Bredin, *The Affair*, 264–265.

37. Bredin, *The Affair*, 383.

Chapter 5. The Climax

1. Bredin, *The Affair*, 213–214.

2. Dreyfus, *Cinq années*, 175.

3. Dreyfus, *Cinq années*, 171.

4. Dreyfus, *Cinq années*, 194.

5. Dreyfus, *Cinq années*, 196.

6. Dreyfus, *Cinq années*, 211.

7. Dreyfus, *Cinq années*, 217.

8. Dreyfus, *Cinq années*, 218.

9. Dreyfus, *Cinq années*, 220–221.

10. "Symptômes," *L'Univers israélite*, December 23, 1898, 422.

11. Blum, *Souvenirs*, 55–56.

12. Joly, *Histoire politique de l'affaire Dreyfus*, 224–225.

13. Joly, *Histoire politique de l'affaire Dreyfus*, 231; Robert Soucy, "Barrès and Fascism," *French Historical Studies* 5:1 (Spring 1967), 78.

14. "La Souscription Henry," *La Libre parole*, December 17, 1898, 1.

15. Stephen Wilson, *Ideology and Experience*, 125.

16. Translated in Bredin, *The Affair*, 350–352.

17. Stephen Wilson, *Ideology and Experience*, 135–142, 144–145; Bredin, *The Affair*, 350.

18. Bredin, *The Affair*, 352.

19. Stephen Wilson, *Ideology and Experience*, 158.

20. These images were signed "Lenepveu," which was most likely a pseudonym. The identity of the artist has never been established.

21. Pierre Birnbaum, *Un Mythe politique: La "République juive,"* *de Léon Blum à Pierre Mendès-France* (Paris: Fayard, 1988).

22. Bredin, *The Affair*, 392.

23. Cited in Joly, *Histoire politique de l'affaire Dreyfus*, 514.

24. Bredin, *The Affair*, 401.

25. Harris, *Dreyfus*, 311; Robert Gauthier, ed., *"Dreyfusards!" Souvenirs de Mathieu Dreyfus et autres inédits, présentés par Robert Gauthier* (Paris: René Julliard, 1965), 206–207.

26. Translated in Wistrich, "Max Nordau and the Dreyfus Affair," 11.

27. Gauthier, *"Dreyfusards!"* 209; Paléologue, *My Secret Diary*, 169.

28. Barrès, *Scènes et doctrines*, 106.

29. Paléologue, *My Secret Diary*, 170.

30. Joseph Reinach, *Histoire de l'affaire Dreyfus*, 2:515.

31. Translated in Bredin, *The Affair*, 411.

32. Bredin, *The Affair*, 414.

33. Harris, *Dreyfus*, 332.

34. Cited in Wistrich, "Max Nordau and the Dreyfus Affair," 11.

35. *La Libre parole*, September 10, 1899, 1.

36. Barrès, *Scènes et doctrines*, 151.

37. *Le Siècle*, September 10, 1899, 1; Clemenceau, "Vers la victoire!" *L'Aurore*, September 10, 1899, 1.

38. Hannah Arendt, "From the Dreyfus Affair to France Today," *Jewish Social Studies* 4:3 (1942), 197.

39. Cited in Ronald K. Huch, "British Reaction to the Dreyfus Affair," *Social Science* 50:1 (Winter 1975), 23–24; Bredin, *The Affair*, 430.

40. "American Attitude Towards Dreyfus," *Atlanta Constitution*, August 19, 1899; cited in Egal Feldman, *The Dreyfus Affair and the American Conscience, 1895–1906* (Detroit: Wayne State University Press, 1981), 110.

41. Carl Schurz, "France After the Zola Trial," *Harper's Weekly*, March 12, 1898, 243; see Feldman, *The Dreyfus Affair*, 97–111.

42. Mark Twain, "Concerning the Jews," *Harper's Magazine*, August 31, 1899, 532.

43. "Verdict Is Against Jews," *New York Times*, September 10, 1899, 2.

44. Feldman, *The Dreyfus Affair*, 102.

45. Ida B. Wells-Barnett, "Lynch Law in America," *Arena*, January 1900, 15–24.

46. W. E. B. DuBois, *The Autobiography of W. E. B. DuBois* (New York: International, 1968), 122.

47. Joseph Reinach, *Histoire de l'affaire Dreyfus*, 2:646.

48. Translated in Bredin, *The Affair*, 433.

49. Dreyfus, *Souvenirs*, 266–267.

50. Burns, *Dreyfus*, 268; Dreyfus, *Souvenirs*, 268.

51. Dreyfus, *Souvenirs*, 269.

52. Joseph Reinach, *Histoire de l'affaire Dreyfus*, 2:666.

53. Translated in Bredin, *The Affair*, 435.

54. Burns, *Dreyfus*, 286

55. Translated in Burns, *Dreyfus*, 288.

56. Burns, *Dreyfus*, 293, 295.

57. Translated in Bredin, *The Affair*, 463.

58. Vincent Duclert, *Alfred Dreyfus: L'honneur d'un patriote* (Paris: Fayard, 2006), 938. This is the original, longer edition.

59. Cited in Duclert, *Alfred Dreyfus* (2006), 951.

60. Duclert, *Alfred Dreyfus* (2006), 952.

61. Cited in Duclert, *Alfred Dreyfus* (2006), 955.

62. "La Rehabilitation de Dreyfus," *Le Siècle*, July 13, 1906, 1.

63. "Justice," *L'Aurore*, July 13, 1906, 1.

64. Georges Joumas, *Alfred Dreyfus, citoyen* (Orléans: Regain de lecture, 2018), 10.

65. Central Consistory Minutes, July 20, 1906, HM 1070, Central Archive for the History of the Jewish People, Jerusalem; cited in Hyman, "The French Jewish Community," 34.

66. Dreyfus, *Souvenirs*, 434–435. Also see Bredin, *The Affair*, 485.

Chapter 6. The Reaction

1. Sholem Aleichem is the pseudonym of Solomon Naumovich Rabinovich. The English translation of the story can be found in *The Best of Sholom* [sic] *Aleichem*, ed. Irving Howe and Ruth R. Wisse (Washington, D.C.: New Republic Books, 1979), 113–116.

The story was originally published in the Yiddish newspaper *Der Fraynd*.

2. Susan Rubin Suleiman, "Entre histoire et 'roman de concierge': L'Affaire Dreyfus dans l'imaginaire populaire des années 1930," *Les Cahiers naturalistes* 76 (2002), 157–176. Suleiman points out that there were two waves of popular novels about the affair, one contemporary with the events and then a revival of interest in the case in the 1930s.

3. "Drayfusl mayn kind," performed by Lifshe Schaechter-Widman, *The Yiddish Song of the Week*, presented by the An-sky Jewish Folklore Research Project, https://yiddishsong.wordpress.com/2011/10/03/drayfusl-mayn-kind-performed-by-lifshe-schaechter -widman, consulted August 4, 2022; Henry A. Russotto, "Dreyfus March Two-Step" [sheet music] (New York: Katzenelenbogen and Rabinowitz, 1899).

4. Moshe Zeifert, *Dreyfus, or The Story of an Innocent Man* [Megiles Dreyfus, oder Di geshikhte fun eyn unshuldigen] (New York: J. Katzenelenbogen, 1899).

5. David Sorkin, *Emancipation Politics: The Jewish Campaign for Rights in Europe and the United States* (forthcoming). Ezra Mendelsohn gives a detailed description of Jewish ideologies in *On Modern Jewish Politics* (New York: Oxford University Press, 1993), however he does not discuss the Dreyfus Affair. Antony Polonsky describes the orthodox reaction to the affair in "The Dreyfus Affair and Polish-Jewish Interaction, 1890–1914," *Jewish History* 11:2 (Fall 1997), 24.

6. Arendt, *Origins of Totalitarianism*, 120.

7. Herzl's statement is translated in Henry J. Cohen, "Theodor Herzl's Conversion to Zionism," *Jewish Social Studies* 32:2 (April 1970), 103. See Derek Penslar, *Theodor Herzl: The Charismatic Leader* (New Haven: Yale University Press, 2020), 68–69.

8. Penslar, *Herzl*, 68–69.

9. Translated in Jess Olson, "The Dreyfus Affair in Early Zionist Culture," in *Revising Dreyfus*, ed. Maya Balakirsky Katz (Leiden: Brill, 2013), 330–331.

10. A.L., "Der Justizirrthum Dreyfus," *Die Welt*, December 29, 1897, 6.

11. Olson, "The Dreyfus Affair in Early Zionist Culture," 320. Christopher E. Forth also describes how the affair led to Herzl's call for Jews to reclaim their masculine honor in *The Dreyfus Affair and the Crisis of French Manhood* (Baltimore: Johns Hopkins University Press, 2004).

12. Translated in Richard I. Cohen, "The Dreyfus Affair and the Jews," in *Antisemitism Through the Ages*, ed. Shmuel Almog (Oxford: Pergamon, 1988), 308.

13. "II Kongressrede, Basel, 28 August 1898," in Max Nordau, *Zionistische Schriften* (Cologne/Leipzig, 1909), 60, translated in Wistrich, "Max Nordau and the Dreyfus Affair," 9.

14. Wistrich, "Max Nordau and the Dreyfus Affair," 11.

15. Nordau, "Das Jahre 1901 in der Weltgeschichte," *Die Neue Freie Presse*, January 1, 1902, 1–7, translated in Wistrich, "Max Nordau and the Dreyfus Affair," 12; and Nordau, *Französische Staatsmänner* (Berlin, 1916), 189–191, translated in Wistrich, "Max Nordau and the Dreyfus Affair," 12.

16. Isidore Cahen, "Sommes-nous défendus?" *Les Archives israélites*, December 27, 1894, 423–424.

17. "A propos des révélations dans *l'Éclair*," *L'Univers israélite*, September 25, 1896, 8.

18. Hippolyte Prague, "Les Juifs et la République," *Les Archives israélites*, March 31, 1898, 99.

19. M.B., "La Crise ministérielle et l'affaire Dreyfus," *L'Univers israélite*, June 23, 1899, 426.

20. The article cited above blamed the Catholic Church for French antisemitism. See also "Das Ende des Zionismus," *Allgemeine Zeitung des Judentums*, February 17, 1899, 78.

21. "Unsere Ehrenpflicht gegen Dreyfus—von Prof. Dr. Hermann Cohen," *Allgemeine Zeitung des Judentums*, June 9, 1899, 268.

22. "Der geschichtliche Sinn des Abschlusses der Dreyfus-Affäre—von Geh. Reg.-Rat Prof. Hermann Cohen," *Allgemeine Zeitung des Judentums*, July 27, 1906, 352.

23. *Izraelita*, April 6, 1898, translated in Polonsky, "The Dreyfus Affair and Polish-Jewish Interaction, 1890–1914," 24.

24. Translated in Polonsky, "The Dreyfus Affair and Polish-Jewish Interaction, 1890–1914," 25.

25. Polonsky, "The Dreyfus Affair and Polish-Jewish Interaction, 1890–1914," 22.

26. *Jewish Chronicle*, December 28, 1894, 5.

27. "Zola on Dreyfus," *Jewish Chronicle*, January 28, 1896, 17.

28. "Dreyfus Condemned," *Jewish Chronicle*, September 15, 1899, 8; "The Triumph of Hate," *Jewish Chronicle*, September 15, 1899, 10.

29. "Dreyfus Condemned," *Jewish Chronicle*, September 15, 1899, 15.

30. "Major Dreyfus," *Jewish Chronicle*, September 21, 1906, 8.

31. "In France," *American Israelite*, December 27, 1894, 6.

32. "Forced to Change Her Name," *American Israelite*, March 28, 1895, 1.

33. *American Israelite*, November 11, 1897, 4.

34. *American Israelite*, June 6, 1895, 4.

35. *American Israelite*, June 6, 1895, 4.

36. *American Israelite*, June 6, 1895, 4.

37. "Jew Baiting in Algeria," *American Israelite*, July 20, 1899, 3.

38. "A Degenerate Nation," *American Israelite*, January 20, 1898. Max Nordau's *Degeneration* was published in 1892 and translated into English in 1896.

39. Feldman, *The Dreyfus Affair*, 6–7, 32.

40. *American Israelite*, April 7, 1899, 4. Several articles mention Zionism in the editorial section.

41. "M. Yves Guyot on Zionism and Anti-Semitism," *American Israelite*, July 27, 1899.

42. *American Israelite*, June 22, 1899, 4. On the proposal to present Dreyfus with a sword, see the *Forverts*, July 12, 1899, 1.

43. "Detroit, MI," *American Israelite*, September 21, 1899, 2.

44. *American Israelite*, July 12, 1906, 4.

45. "Dreyfus Redivivus," *American Israelite*, July 19, 1906, 4.

46. *American Israelite*, July 19, 1906, 1.

47. *American Israelite*, August 2, 1906, 4.

48. "France," *American Israelite*, September 20, 1906, 1.

49. Nancy L. Green, "Socialist Anti-Semitism, Defense of a Bourgeois Jew, and Discovery of the Jewish Proletariat," *International Review of Social History* 30:3 (December 1985), 375.

50. Marrus, *Politics of Assimilation*, 247–249.

51. "Le Judaïsme et le socialisme, Deuxième article," *L'Univers israélite*, May 9, 1899, 267–268.

52. Translated in Pierre Birnbaum, *Léon Blum: Prime Minister, Socialist, Zionist*, trans. Arthur Goldhammer (New Haven: Yale University Press, 2015), 55.

53. Birnbaum, *Léon Blum*, 56–58.

54. Jonathan Frankel, *Prophecy and Politics: Socialism, Nationalism, and the Russian Jews, 1862–1917* (Cambridge: Cambridge University Press, 1981), 222.

55. Frankel, *Prophecy and Politics*, 466.

56. Frankel, *Prophecy and Politics*, 467.

57. All the pieces by Cahan are collected in *Grandma Never Lived in America: The New Journalism of Abraham Cahan*, ed. Moses Rischin (Bloomington: Indiana University Press, 1985), 36–42.

58. Frankel, *Prophecy and Politics*, 468–469. Also see Matthew Frye Jacobson, *Special Sorrows: The Diasporic Imagination of Irish, Polish, and Jewish Immigrants in the United States* (Berkeley: University of California Press, 2002), especially 62–64.

59. See, for example, "Dreyfuses teus," January 15, 1899, 1; and "A neyer trayl far Dreyfusen offitzyel brikhtet," May 30, 1899, 1–2.

60. See, for example: "Madam Dreyfuses fertsveyflung," March 1, 1898, 1; and "Dreyfuses biterer un miaumser meus," June 9, 1899, 1. Articles referring to Dreyfus's health were very numerous: for example, the coverage of the affair on June 28, July 14, July 28, September 13, and September 22, 1899.

61. Frankel, *Prophecy and Politics*, 466–473.

62. "Jacob lived in the land where his father had stayed, the land of Canaan," *Kol Mahazike ha-dat*, December 7, 1906.

63. Jonathan Frankel argues that the antisemitic crises of the Damascus Affair of 1840, the Mortara kidnapping of 1858, the Russian pogroms of 1881–1882, and the Dreyfus Affair all played

a crucial role in forming modern Jewish political identity; Frankel, "Crisis as a Factor in Modern Jewish Politics, 1840 and 1881–82," in *Living with Antisemitism: Modern Jewish Responses*, ed. Jehuda Reinharz (Waltham, Mass.: Brandeis University Press, 1987), 42–58.

64. "Dreyfus Condemned," *Jewish Chronicle*, September 15, 1899, 15.

65. Benedict Anderson, *Imagined Communities: Reflections on the Origin and Spread of Nationalism* (New York: Verso, 1983).

Chapter 7. The Aftermath

1. Burns, *Dreyfus*, 311.

2. Alfred Dreyfus, *Carnets (1899–1907)* (Paris: Calmann-Lévy, 1998), 273; Joumas, *Alfred Dreyfus*, 13.

3. Letter to the marquise Arconati-Visconti, cited in Joumas, *Alfred Dreyfus*, 15.

4. Neville, *Dreyfus intime*, 73.

5. Joumas, *Alfred Dreyfus*, 20–21.

6. BN, NAF 24909, translated in Burns, *Dreyfus*, 348.

7. Jaumas, *Alfred Dreyfus*, 54–56.

8. Cited in Duclert, *Alfred Dreyfus*, 608; Burns, *Dreyfus*, 337.

9. Burns, *Dreyfus*, 364.

10. Burns, *Dreyfus*, 389, 398.

11. Alfred Dreyfus, *Souvenirs et correspondance*, 442–445; Burns, *Dreyfus*, 427–430.

12. Jean Daniel reports hearing Levinas quote his father in *La Prison juive* (Paris: Odile Jacob, 2003), 68.

13. Élisabeth Weissman, *Lucie Dreyfus, la femme du capitaine* (Paris: Textuel, 2015), 312–313.

14. Harris, *Dreyfus*, 286–292; Alfred Dreyfus, *Lettres à la marquise* (Paris: Grasset & Fasquelle, 2017).

15. Joumas, *Alfred Dreyfus*, 65.

16. Translated in Burns, *Dreyfus*, 328.

17. Olson, "The Dreyfus Affair in Early Zionist Culture," 315–317.

18. "Gedanken über den Zionismus, von Alfred Dreyfus," trans. J.Z., *Die Welt*, January 31, 1902, 5. The editor notes that the article

is a German translation of an English-language article that appeared in the New Year's edition of Hearst's *New York Journal*.

19. Burns, *Dreyfus*, 433–434.

20. Alfred Dreyfus, *Souvenirs et correspondance*, 445–446.

21. Duclert, *Alfred Dreyfus*, 633.

22. "Mort d'Alfred Dreyfus," *L'Action française*, July 13, 1935, 2.

23. "Mort du lieutenant-colonel Dreyfus," *Le Temps*, July 14, 1935; cited in Duclert, *Alfred Dreyfus*, 629–630.

24. Blum, *Souvenirs*, 33.

25. Léon Daudet, "Le Cabinet Blum et la question juive," *L'Action française*, May 17, 1936, translated in Birnbaum, *Léon Blum*, 1–2.

26. Burns, *Dreyfus*, 470.

27. Burns, *Dreyfus*, 473–475.

28. Burns, *Dreyfus*, 481–483.

29. In 1994, as part of the centenary commemoration of the Dreyfus Affair, the army commissioned a report that stated only that "the innocence of Captain Dreyfus was the thesis generally admitted by historians," giving the false impression that his innocence remained in doubt. When a journalist for *Libération* revealed the content of the report, the army felt obliged to declare formally that Dreyfus was innocent. Zemmour might have been thinking of the army's report when he made his statement regarding Dreyfus's innocence. On the centenary of the affair, see Duclert, *Alfred Dreyfus*, 652–653.

ACKNOWLEDGMENTS

My thanks go first to my editor Ileene Smith and to the Jewish Lives series editors Anita Shapira and Steven J. Zipperstein for offering me the opportunity to pursue a long-standing interest in Alfred Dreyfus. Sarah Chalfant and Rebecca Nagel of the Wylie Agency provided astute guidance throughout the process. A fellowship at the Cullman Center of the New York Public Library gave me the time and space to write, and I'm extremely grateful to the interim director Martha Hodes, to the Cullman Center staff, and to my fellow fellows for their provocative questions and stimulating discussions about the project.

I took a class on the literature of the Dreyfus Affair from Susan Suleiman in graduate school thirty years ago and have never stopped learning from her. Her comments on the entire manuscript—along with those of Alice Kaplan, Ghita Schwarz, and David Sorkin— made it infinitely better. Alice Kaplan suggested I write this book and spent countless hours discussing it with me. Sarah Maza and Jennifer Siegel offered wonderful feedback on key sections. Nicola

Angeli, McKinzie Crozier, Yoni Dabas, and Lea Jouannais Weiler helped me with the research, especially the coverage of the affair in the Jewish press. David A. Bell, Shira Billet, Pierre Birnbaum, Howard Bloch, Dominique Brancher, Carolyn Dean, David Geller, Lawrence Kritzman, Joshua Lambert, James McAuley, Joshua Price, Pierre Saint-Amand, Eliyahu Stern, Gillian Thomas, Francesca Trivellato, Laura van Straaten, and Caroline Weber offered valuable support along the way. Librarians at institutions around the world could not have been more gracious, especially Rachel Koskas and Judith Lindemann (Musée d'art et d'histoire du Judaïsme, Paris), John Pollack (Lorraine Beitler Collection, University of Pennsylvania Library), and Lyudmila Sholokhova and Jeanne-Marie Musto (Dorot Division at the New York Public Library). Heather Gold, Phillip King, and Noreen O'Connor-Abel of Yale University Press were a pleasure to work with. And I'm enormously grateful to my other friends and family for helping me through the five years of my life it took to write this book.

INDEX

Page numbers in italic type refer to illustrations

197

antisemitism (*continued*)
of Defense Against Antisemitism,
77; and denunciations of Dreyfus, 1; Dreyfusards and anti-
Dreyfusard coalitions and, 93;
Dreyfus's attitude toward, 42–43,
131–132, 165; and Dreyfus's
court-martial, 42, 45, 47–49, 53,
54, 56, 71–72, 180n57; at Dreyfus's degradation ceremony, 56,
137, 139, 180n57; and Dreyfus's
school experiences, 19; Dreyfus's
second court-martial and, 121;
and efforts to free Dreyfus from
prison, 50, 55; Esterhazy and, 93,
94–95; in France, 35–45; French
army and, 31–32, 39, 43–45, 71;
High Court of Appeal and, 131;
Jewish responses to, 41–42, 71,
77; "Jewish syndicate," myth of,
3, 71, 73, 77, 90, 91, 95, 113; and
La Rochelle train station crowd,
60; legislative proposals and,
71–72; modernizing trend, as
reaction to, 36, 44, 46, 48; Museum of Horrors posters, 115,
116, 124, 125; Nazis, Holocaust,
and World War II, 5, 63, 74, 114,
122, 136, 156, 163–164, 167–170;
as political issue, 99–100, 101,
115–117; of the press, 38–41, *40*,
46, 71, 160–161, 166, 170; and
racialization of Jewishness, 38,
102; of Socialists, 36, 37, 78,
94–95, 150–151; as unifying force
for Jews, 156–157, 191–192n63;
Zola and, 72, 93–94
Antisemitism: Its History and Its Causes
(Lazare), 78–80
appeals: for first court-martial, denied,
60; High Court of Appeal and,
106–107, 109–110, 130–132;
Lucie Dreyfus and, 87, 106;
petitions for, 87, 101–102, 106;
request for revision of judgment,
109–110, 126, 128, 130

Archives israélites, Les (newspaper), 28,
41, 75–76, 141–142, 176n29
Arconati-Visconti, Marquise, 164
Arendt, Hannah, 27, 30, 41, 74, 80,
122, 137, 178n15
L'Argent (Money; Zola), 94
Arnold, Benedict, 144
assassinations, attempted: of Dreyfus,
161–162; of Dreyfus's lawyer,
120–121; of Zola, 161
assimilation, and integration, 3–4, 11,
26–30
Assumptionists, 38, 53
Atlanta Constitution, 123
L'Aurore (newspaper), 94, 96, 102, 122,
132
Auschwitz-Birkenau, 169–170, 172
Autobiography (Du Bois), 125

Balzac, Honoré de, 19
Barrès, Maurice, 48, 92, 102, 103,
112–113, 119, 122
Bastian, Marie (cleaning woman and
spy), 45–46, 82
Baudoin, Manuel, 131
Baur, Marie (later Dreyfus; daughter-
in-law), 160
Begley, Louis, 7
Bertillon, Alphonse, 47, 59, 103
Birnbaum, Pierre, 98, 101, 152
Bismarck, Otto von, 16, 17
Black Death, 9
Blum, Léon, 6, 74, 92, 112, 152, 167
Boisdeffre, Raoul de, 34, 35, 84–85,
89, 91, 103, 104, 106
Bonnefond, Pierre de, 31, 44
bordereau: discovery of, 45–46; in
Dreyfus court-martial, 45–48,
52, 71; Esterhazy's handwriting
matched with, 84, 90, 92–93;
press releases of, 89, 90; at Zola
libel trial, 103
Bourges, artillery school in, 24
Bourget, Paul, 103
boycotts, of France, 125, 148
Brazili (*Ha-Melits* writer), 139

68–69, 85–86; release from,
110–111, 126–127; on Royal
Island, 61–62
—writings: *Cinq années de ma vie*
(Five Years of My Life), 64,
79; *Souvenirs* (Recollections),
42, 126, 159; "Thoughts on
Zionism," 165
Dreyfus, Camille, 76
Dreyfus, Émile (nephew), 162
Dreyfus, Emma, 144–145
Dreyfus, Henriette (sister; later Vala-
brègue), 15, 18, 19–20, 126–127
Dreyfus, Jacob/Jacques (grandfather),
12, 15
Dreyfus, Jacques (brother), 15, 17, 18
Dreyfus, Jeanne (daughter; later Lévy),
30, 34, 127, 160, 162, 168
Dreyfus, Jeannette Libmann (Adèle
Weill; mother), 15, 18, 24,
174n8
Dreyfus, Léon (brother), 15, 18
Dreyfus, Louise (sister), 15, 18
Dreyfus, Lucie Hadamard (wife), 25;
correspondence with Dreyfus
in prison, 28, 31, 53, 55–56, 60,
65–66, 70, 85, 109–110, 164;
death of, 169; efforts on behalf
of Dreyfus in prison, 63, 69–70;
harassed by military authorities,
51, 69–70; hoping to accompany
Dreyfus into exile, 55, 60, 61, 70;
and Jewish education of children,
160; and Jewish philanthropy,
163–164; letters of support received by, 101; marriage to Dreyfus, 24–26, 30, 34, 77; petitions
for reversal of verdict, 87, 106;
popular Jewish interest in, 135,
155; prison visits to Dreyfus, 55,
61; religious faith and practice
of, 28, 29; reunited with Dreyfus
after imprisonment, 111, 127; in
World War I, 162; in World War
II, 168–169
Dreyfus, Marguerite (Magui; niece;
later Reinach), 160, 176n39

Dreyfus, Marie Baur (daughter-in-
law), 160
Dreyfus, Mathieu (brother): burned in
effigy, 96; childhood and education, 15, 18, 19, 26, 30; efforts on
behalf of Dreyfus in prison, 77,
78–79; escape rumor planted by,
85; estrangement of some Dreyfusards from, 129; and initial
defense of Dreyfus, 51, 70–71;
and Lazare pamphlet, 89; match-
ing of Esterhazy's handwriting
with *bordereau*, 92–93; medium
consulted by, 82; and pardon and
release of Dreyfus, 126; reunion
with Dreyfus, 111; Scheurer-
Kestner gives information to,
91, 93; at second court-martial
in Rennes, 117–118, 119, 121;
testifies at trial of Dreyfus's
attempted assassin, 161
Dreyfus, Pierre (son), 30, 34, 42, 127,
160, 162, 164, 165, 168
Dreyfus, Rachel, later Schil (sister), 15,
18, 42–43
Dreyfus, Raphaël (father), 12–15, *14*,
17–18, 26, 34
Dreyfus Affair, 82–107; anti-Dreyfus
and antisemitic riots, 98–101,
109, 141, 151, 156; antisemitism,
centrality of, 4–5, 32, 88, 97–101,
113–115; appeal and overturn-
ing of guilty verdict, 106–107,
109–110, 130–132, 193n29;
coalescence of, 87–88; court-
martial and acquittal of Esterhazy for espionage, 95–96, 97,
109, 111; documents forged
by Henry, 88–89, 90, 91, 104,
105–106, 119, 130; Dreyfusards
and anti-Dreyfusard coalitions
in, 87, 93–95, 98–103, 111–115,
127–128; Dreyfus's ignorance
regarding, 109; intellectuals and,
101–103; escape rumor, 85–86;
Esterhazy's handwriting matched
with *bordereau*, 84, 90, 92–93;

INDEX

Esterhazy, Ferdinand Walsin, 41–42,
83, 88, 135; *bordereau*, handwriting matched with, 84, 90, 92–93;
court-martial and acquittal for
espionage, 95–96, 97, 109, 111;
Dreyfus learns of treachery of,
110; French army officers pro-
tecting, 91; Picquart's investigation of, 83–85, 91; public
exposure as true spy, 93; at Zola
libel trial, 103, 104
Étienne, Eugène, 158

Fabre, Pierre, 47
Faure, Félix, 68–69, 106, 115
Félix, Rachel, 12
Ferris wheel, 130
Figaro, Le (newspaper), 72, 85, 94, 96,
180n57
Fitch, Nancy, 101
Flammarion (publisher), 38
Fontainebleau, artillery training school
at, 21
food, rations and supply parcels,
62–63, 66–67
Forverts (newspaper), 110, 148,
153–155
Forzinetti, Ferdinand, 42, 50, 52
France: antisemitism in, 35–45; boycotts, international calls for, 125,
148; death penalty in, 55, 61;
divorce, legalization of, 72; Dreyfus family and French citizenship
after Franco-Prussian War,
17–18; "Dreyfus in Kasrilevke,"
Jewish attitudes toward France
in, 136; Dreyfusard versus anti-
Dreyfusard conceptions of, 102;
Dreyfus's return to, 110–111;
government of republican defense, 115, 128, 140; immigration
of Jews from Germany to,
163–164; political crises caused
by Dreyfus Affair in, 2, 4, 8,
87–88, 102, 103, 106, 115–117,
125; religious tolerance in, 9–10;
riots, anti-Dreyfus and anti-

semitic, 98–101, 109, 141, 151,
156; separation of church and
state in, 128–129, 149; Socialist
movement in, 150–152; stem-
ming of right-wing nationalist
tide by Dreyfus Affair in, 5, 7;
universal equality, Dreyfus and,
31–32; voting rights for women
in, 11
France, Anatole, 101, 103
France juive, La (Jewish France; Drumont), 37–38, 39, 95
Franco-Judaism, 3, 4, 28–30
Franco-Prussian War (1870–1871),
16–18, 20, 24
Frankel, Jonathan, 152–154
French army: antisemitism and, 31–32,
39, 43–45, 71; artillery versus
cavalry corps, acceptance of Jews
in, 21–22, 41; court-martial of
Esterhazy for espionage, 95;
cover-ups by officers of, 84–85,
88, 89, 91, 93, 96, 97, 110,
127–128; degradation ceremony,
55–58, 57, 137, 139, 180n57;
Dreyfus, career in, 21–24, 31–34,
43–45; Dreyfus compared with
other officers, 23; Dreyfus exonerated and reintegrated in,
132–133, 158–159, 193n29;
Dreyfus's resignation from,
159; Dreyfus's return to service
in World War I, 162; Franco-
Prussian War and, 16–17; general amnesty proposal, 127–128;
General Staff, 31–34, 43–45, 46;
Jews serving in, 20, 43–44;
Mathieu Dreyfus in, 19; second
court-martial in Rennes, military
judges' control of, 117; Statistical
Section (intelligence division),
45–47, 54, 82, 83, 86, 88–90;
Zola libel trial and, 103–105
French Forces of the Interior (World
War II), 169
French Revolution, 4, 10, 11, 21, 26,
28, 36–37, 87, 92

INDEX

JEWISH LIVES is a prizewinning series of interpretive biography designed to explore the many facets of Jewish identity. Individual volumes illuminate the imprint of Jewish figures upon literature, religion, philosophy, politics, cultural and economic life, and the arts and sciences. Subjects are paired with authors to elicit lively, deeply informed books that explore the range and depth of the Jewish experience from antiquity to the present.

Jewish Lives is a partnership of Yale University Press and the Leon D. Black Foundation. Ileene Smith is editorial director. Anita Shapira and Steven J. Zipperstein are series editors.

Peggy Guggenheim: The Shock of the Modern, by Francine Prose
Ben Hecht: Fighting Words, Moving Pictures, by Adina Hoffman
Heinrich Heine: Writing the Revolution, by George Prochnik
Lillian Hellman: An Imperious Life, by Dorothy Gallagher
Herod the Great: Jewish King in a Roman World, by Martin Goodman
Theodor Herzl: The Charismatic Leader, by Derek Penslar
Abraham Joshua Heschel: A Life of Radical Amazement,
    by Julian Zelizer
Houdini: The Elusive American, by Adam Begley
Jabotinsky: A Life, by Hillel Halkin
Jacob: Unexpected Patriarch, by Yair Zakovitch
Franz Kafka: The Poet of Shame and Guilt, by Saul Friedländer
Rav Kook: Mystic in a Time of Revolution, by Yehudah Mirsky
Stanley Kubrick: American Filmmaker, by David Mikics
Stan Lee: A Life in Comics, by Liel Leibovitz
Primo Levi: The Matter of a Life, by Berel Lang
Maimonides: Faith in Reason, by Alberto Manguel
Groucho Marx: The Comedy of Existence, by Lee Siegel
Karl Marx: Philosophy and Revolution, by Shlomo Avineri
Golda Meir: Israel's Matriarch, by Deborah E. Lipstadt
Menasseh ben Israel: Rabbi of Amsterdam, by Steven Nadler
Moses Mendelssohn: Sage of Modernity, by Shmuel Feiner
Harvey Milk: His Lives and Death, by Lillian Faderman
Arthur Miller: American Witness, by John Lahr
Moses: A Human Life, by Avivah Gottlieb Zornberg
Amos Oz: Writer, Activist, Icon, by Robert Alter
Proust: The Search, by Benjamin Taylor
Yitzhak Rabin: Soldier, Leader, Statesman, by Itamar Rabinovich
Walther Rathenau: Weimar's Fallen Statesman, by Shulamit Volkov
Man Ray: The Artist and His Shadows, by Arthur Lubow
Sidney Reilly: Master Spy, by Benny Morris
Admiral Hyman Rickover: Engineer of Power, by Marc Wortman

Jerome Robbins: A Life in Dance, by Wendy Lesser
Julius Rosenwald: Repairing the World, by Hasia R. Diner
Mark Rothko: Toward the Light in the Chapel, by Annie Cohen-Solal
Ruth: A Migrant's Tale, by Ilana Pardes
Gershom Scholem: Master of the Kabbalah, by David Biale
Bugsy Siegel: The Dark Side of the American Dream,
    by Michael Shnayerson
Solomon: The Lure of Wisdom, by Steven Weitzman
Steven Spielberg: A Life in Films, by Molly Haskell
Spinoza: Freedom's Messiah, by Ian Buruma
Alfred Stieglitz: Taking Pictures, Making Painters, by Phyllis Rose
Barbra Streisand: Redefining Beauty, Femininity, and Power,
    by Neal Gabler
Henrietta Szold: Hadassah and the Zionist Dream,
    by Francine Klagsbrun
Leon Trotsky: A Revolutionary's Life, by Joshua Rubenstein
Warner Bros: The Making of an American Movie Studio,
    by David Thomson
Elie Wiesel: Confronting the Silence, by Joseph Berger

FORTHCOMING TITLES INCLUDE:

Abraham, by Anthony Julius
Hannah Arendt, by Masha Gessen
The Ba'al Shem Tov, by Ariel Mayse
Walter Benjamin, by Peter Gordon
Franz Boas, by Noga Arikha
Bob Dylan, by Sasha Frere-Jones
Anne Frank, by Ruth Franklin
George Gershwin, by Gary Giddins
Ruth Bader Ginsburg, by Jeffrey Rosen
Jesus, by Jack Miles